A Wandering Tribe

Dispersal of the Catawba Nation
1800 to 1900

S. Pony Hill

Published by Backintyme Publishing

Crofton, Ky. U.S.A.

Copyright @2016
ALL RIGHTS RESERVED

Backintyme Publishing
1341 Grapevine Rd.
Crofton, KY. 42217
270-985-8568
Email Backintyme@mehrapublishing.com

Printed in the United States of America
June 2018

ISBN: 9780939479498
Library of Congress Control Number: 2016950485

A Wandering Tribe

Dispersal of the Catawba Nation

1800 to 1900

S. Pony Hill

Table of Contents

Table of Contents vi
Acknowledgments viii
Introduction ix
Major Catawba Out-Migrations 1
    1730-1760 2
    Revolutionary War 3
    1830-1850 7
    1880-1900 10
FAMILY SKETCHES 11
    BROWN 11
    BUNCH 15
    CANTY 17
    CLARK 21
    COLE 23
    EADY 31
    EVANS 35
    FLOWERS 45
    GENTRY 47
    GIBBS 49
    GOINS/GOINGS 51
    GORDON 55
    GUY 57
    HARRIS 69
    HART 73
    HEAD 75
    JEFFRIES 83
    JOHNSON 87
    KEGG 89
    KENNEDY 93
    LERBLANCE 103
    LOGAN 107
    LUCAS 107

MORRISON 109
PATTERSON 111
RED HEAD 113
ROBBINS 115
SCOTT 117
SIZEMORE 125
STEPHENS 129
TAYLOR 131
TIMS 139
TYLER 143
WATTS 145
Appendix 1 149
BEAUFORT DISTRICT INDIAN SETTLEMENT 149
BEAMER 163
BING 166
BOZZARD 170
BUSBY 170
HENSON 174
JACKSON 175
JONES: 175
MIMS 176
WILLIAMS 176
Appendix 2 179
WESTERN CATAWBA INDIAN ASSOCIATION 179
Appendix 3 189
Revolutionary War Paylist of 1780: 189
Petition of "the Chief and Head Men of Cataba Nation" 190
A List of Names of Catawba Indians, residing in South Carolina 193
A List of Names of Catawba Indians, residing in South Carolina 193
INDEX 195

Acknowledgments

In this modern era of research, dominated by the internet, search engines, and massive ancestry websites, no amount of research is conducted in a vacuum. The electronic age has allowed instantaneous communication with other researchers and the rapid sharing of information at a speed unheralded in history. Like all students of southeastern Native research, I too owe a great debt of gratitude to a host of early scholars like Brewton Berry, Calvin Beale, McDonald Furman, Frank G Speck, and Robert K Thomas. Invaluable documentation and information has been, and continues to be, rescued from obscurity by such heroes as Forest Hazel, Thomas Blumer, Judy Canty Martin, Kianga Lucas, and Wes Taukchiray. Without dedicated pioneers such as these plowing the rocky fields of history, leaving the fertile soil loose enough to extract the documentary jewels long lost to dusty archives, publications such as this one would not be possible.

Equal gratitude goes out to the numerous descendants of the Bing, Brown, Busby, Canty, Chavers, Clark, Eady, Evans, Gentry, Gibbs, Goins, Guy, Harris, Head, Jeffries, Kennedy, Lerblance, Patterson, Taylor, Tims, Tyler, and Watts families who so graciously allowed their family pictures to be displayed within these pages. These priceless portraits are the spice on top of what would otherwise be a very dry meal.

Introduction

Much has been written regarding the Catawba Nation. Their near constant historic state of warfare with both the Cherokee and other Iroquoian tribes further north, their reliable militaristic support for their white neighbors, and their multi-generational struggle to maintain their land base, have been the subject of numerous manuscripts. While thousands of pages have been dedicated to memorializing the history of the tribe, and an equal amount of parchment devoted to the Indians who resided on the Catawba reservation, the pen of the historian has remained silent on one major aspect of the Catawba experience: those Indian families and individuals who left the reservation. Given that, by all accounts, the entire Catawba tribe was absent from the reservation at a minimum of twice between the Eighteenth and Nineteenth centuries, and also several periods where at least half the Catawba population were absentee, it's surprising that this subject hasn't been the target of greater study. I hope to do my part to rectify that oversight with this book.

We know from various accounts that between 1700 and 1800 the population of the Catawba reservation decreased by more than fifty percent. At least half of this decrease was due to the mortality of old age, accident, or disease, however a significant portion of population reduction was certainly that these Indians did what any human population would do when pressed by disease, failing crops, raiding parties of foreign tribes, and creeping land loss due to the subtle designs of encroaching settlement: they left the confines of the reservation to explore life in other areas. Between 1800 and 1900 the already halved reservation population was again carved down, this time by nearly three quarters and almost entirely due to outmigration.

What happened to those three quarters of the tribe who abandoned their ancient homeland? Where did they ultimately settle down? Did they continue to self-Identify as Catawba or, in some respects even more importantly, were they recorded as "Catawba" or even as "Indian" by the census enumerator, tax collector, or court officials in these new areas? Unfortunately, the "official" records, i.e. census enumerations, county tax rolls, and the like, do little to answer these questions.

When I first struck out to formally encapsulate the documentation of these Catawba descendant families, I knew that a host of historic factors weighed heavily against the proper identification of these individuals as "Indian", at least within the official records. For much of the early Nineteenth century, census enumerators were given detailed instructions regarding who would be considered "Indian" as far as the U.S. census was concerned. To meet this criterion an individual must have been (1) regarded as having majority Indian blood, (2) regarded as being an "Indian" within the community in which they lived, (3) not subject to local or state taxation, and (4) currently resided on a "known Indian reservation." If a person met all of these criteria, then that individual was an "Indian" and, as far as the census was concerned, was not to be recorded. If a person did not fall within one or more of the aforementioned criteria the regular practice was to record the person's "race" based on their local taxation status.

During the mid to late Nineteenth century the majority of states had refined their taxation, legal, and even less documented 'social', codes to declare that a person of "less than one quarter Indian descent" would meet the legal threshold of being "white." Persons "colored by Indian blood of more than one grandparent" were to be taxed, legally recorded, and "in all other ways regarded as a mulatto" (of course, in the 1800's the term "mulatto" was used differently than we perceive the term today. In that era "Mulatto" was used more in line with its root definition, i.e. "a mule," or any half-breed, and was commonly used to describe any number of racial mixtures). An individual could live within the confines of a well-known Native community and be recorded as "Indian", then move to southern Georgia and be recorded as "white", then cross the border into Alabama and be recorded as a "mulatto." This resulted in the haphazard "race" designations that even the most casual of readers will easily observe reflected on the census records included within this publication.

As these Indian blooded families spread out across the Southeast and Midwest, they found themselves increasingly challenged to carve out a "third race" niche within an increasingly bifurcated legal and social structure. Claiming to be "Indian" within a society that recognized only "black" or "white," these Catawba descendants were without question continuously viewed with suspicion by their white neighbors. As Jim Crow gained a chokehold on the populace, at best they found their indigenous ancestry repeatedly tested if they took on white spouses and, at worst, directly denied if their spouses were negro. Given the hypervigilant racially bifurcated environment in which these scattered Indian families found themselves, it's a wonder that *any* documentation of their Native claims found its way into the "official" records, and truly a miracle that documentation of this "Indian" self-identification survived at all.

One thing that *does* stand out, even in the midst of woefully incomplete records, is that these Catawba descendants indeed maintained their public identity as "Indian" and, in a surprisingly large amount, preserved their ancient tribal origin. My hope is that this book, in some small way, pays tribute to the strength, pride and perseverance that these Catawba descendants demonstrated without the benefit of a reservation boundary line.

Major Catawba Out-Migrations

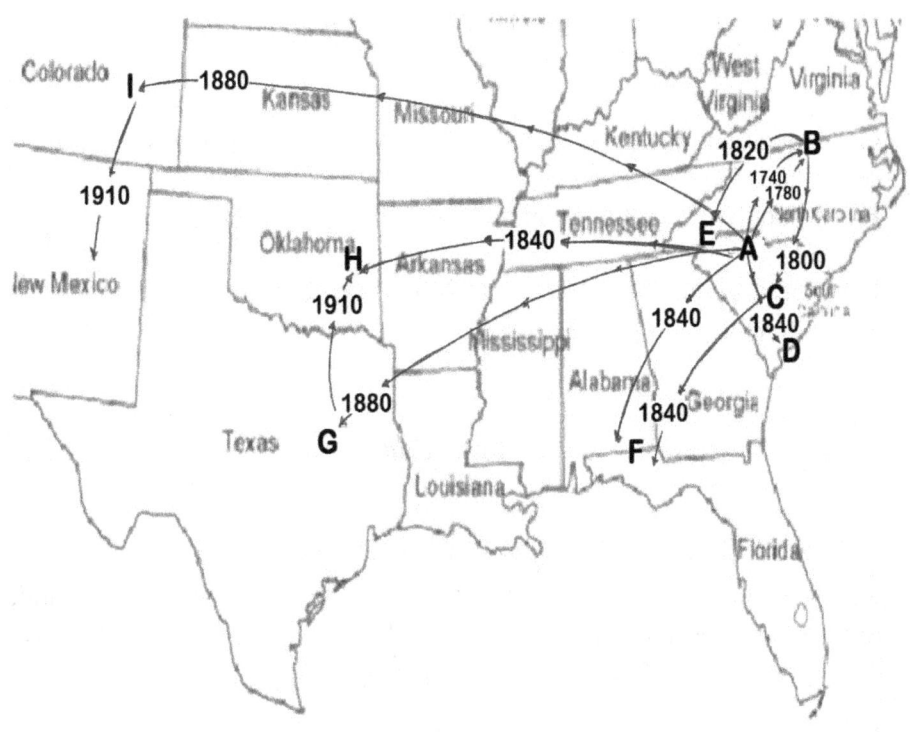

Major Catawba Outmigration 1730 to 1900

A: Catawba Reservation, South Carolina

B: North Carolina/Virginia Border (1740's small groups with Saponi & Cheraw – 1780's entire tribe during the Revolutionary War)

C: Sumter County, South Carolina (1790's with Cheraw from Halifax County, NC)

D: Beaufort District, South Carolina (1840's from Catawba Reservation, SC)

A Wandering Tribe

E: Macon County, North Carolina (1820's with Saponi from Orange County, NC)

F: Alabama/Florida Border (1840's from Catawba Reservation & Sumter County, SC)

G: Cooke County, Texas (1880's from Catawba Reservation, SC)

H: Indian Territory/Oklahoma (1840's from Cherokee, NC)

I: Colorado/Utah/New Mexico (1880's from Catawba Reservation, SC with Mormon missionaries)

1730-1760

Between 1730 and 1740, groups of Cheraw, Pee Dee, Saponi, and Waxhaw Indians, pressured by waves of white settlers moving inland, abandoned their ancient homes and took up residence among the Catawba. This was not an unusual occurrence as the tribes spoke a language similar to the Catawba, all comprising an eastern linguistic and cultural branch of the Dakota Sioux.

As fate would have it, they were not the only new arrival at the forested reservation. Smallpox swept through the villages of the Catawba, Saponi, Cheraw, Pee Dee, and other smaller tribes who had sought refuge on the banks of the Catawba River. Within a year, some have estimated, more than one half of the Native residents of the reservation had perished from the dreaded disease.

The surviving Saponi Indians gathered their possessions and returned to the Virginia-North Carolina border accompanied by some Cheraw and a few Catawba. Upon arriving at their old lands between the Roanoke and Meherrin, they petitioned Lt. Governor Gooch for

Major Catawba Out-Migrations

permission to resettle in Virginia, which was granted in 1733. It is this same era that surnames which had become common among the Catawba, namely Evans, Harris, and Scott, would begin appearing in such Virginia/North Carolina border counties as Brunswick and Mecklenburg. The several Scott families of Sumter, South Carolina who, within less than a generation, returned from Halifax to South Carolina and strongly claimed to be "Catawba," are undoubtedly a result of this wave of northward migration.

During this same period a sizeable body of Pee Dee Indians, who had earlier been drawn to the Catawba Reservation by the appeals of the Catawba leadership, also left the reservation. Either due to the aforementioned rampant smallpox, or realizing their vulnerable position remaining within reach of raiding parties of northern tribes, they petitioned South Carolina legislators to allow them to move "closer to the settlements." Permission was given, and the Pee Dee settled just north of Charleston, on a 100-acre reservation set aside for them near the lands of James Coachman.

In 1753 the Catawba requested that the South Carolinians persuade the Pee Dee to return north; the Pee Dee, however, would not budge. Certainly numerous Pee Dee had intermarried with, or otherwise influenced, several Catawba to join their southern resettlement, as this likely explains the Catawba origin affidavits of the Bing, Busby, Eady and other Indian mixed blood families of Berkeley and Beaufort Districts.

Revolutionary War

The Catawba Indians, and the smaller remnant tribes allied with them, were immediately sympathetic to the Patriot cause. The Indians were as equally displeased as the colonists regarding the bureaucracy and corruption of a government far across the sea, and were more amiable

A Wandering Tribe

to dealing face-to-face with their white neighbors. When General George Washington sent a personally written letter to the Catawba requesting their assistance against the British, the Indians gladly answered the call.

In the early phases of the Revolutionary War the so called "Southern Campaign" was a disaster for the Americans. Charleston fell and British forces, the world's most advanced military force at the time, were marching north. When British forces advanced far enough to occupy Camden, the Continental forces under General Sumter pulled back and established camps on the Catawba reservation land.

Now, seeing their friends and fellow soldiers repeatedly routed by the British, news filtered in that the Redcoats had massacred over 100 Continental soldiers who had surrendered at the Waxhaws, the Catawba became aware of the danger their wives and children faced if the British progressed as far as the Catawba River.

In August of 1780 the Catawba warriors rounded up all of their women, children and elderly. The entire Catawba Nation abandoned their reservation and slowly made their way north. The long procession of Indians walking alongside their loaded down packhorses made their way first to Charlotte and then to Salisbury. Just north of Salisbury the Indians parted ways with the main body of Carolina settlers fleeing north. History remains silent on where the Catawba women, children and elderly spent that year of exile, except that they found shelter with "a friendly tribe."

There can be no doubt that the Catawba families had never lost touch with their relatives who had removed to the Virginia/North Carolina border country with the Saponi and Cheraw. While the majority of the Catawba returned to their reservation within the year, there is also no question a few remained in the north among their relatives. William Guy and Simon Jeffries, the forefathers of a "remnant of the tribe of

Major Catawba Out-Migrations

Catawba Indians" who had joined the Patriot cause from their homes along the Virginia/North Carolina border, were undeniably progeny of the Nation's flight north before the war machine of the Redcoats.

In addition to the Catawba who had enlisted with the Continentals from their South Carolina reservation, numerous Indian blooded men volunteered from their homes along the Virginia/North Carolina line (namely Halifax and Granville Counties of North Carolina, and Brunswick and Greenville Counties of Virginia), the same place the aforementioned "friendly tribe" was said to reside. Several of these men were transferred from the North Carolina Continental Line to the South Carolina forces under General Sumter, training extensively in the High Hills of Santee, the same area the South Carolina Legislature would soon gift General Sumter 2,560 acres for his exemplary service to the state.

The service of Catawba warriors under General Sumter was extensive and well documented. On June 21st, Thomas Drennan, South Carolina Indian Agent to the Catawba Indians, submitted a "Pay bill for Cap. Thomas Drennans company of Catawba Indians under the command of Genr. Thomas Sumpter in the State of South Carolina Service for the year 1780 and discharge in the year 1781." Drennan listed Catawba Indians: "General New River, John Brown, Robbin, Willis (deceased killed at Rock Mtn his wife and child alive), Suggar Jamey, Pinetree George, John Morrison, Henry White, John Cagg, Captain Quash, Little Mick, Patrick Redhead, Billey Williams, Big Jamey, Billey Cagg, John Connar, Doctor John, Chunkey Pipe, Capt Petter, Billey Otter, Little Aleck, Colonel John Eayrs, Petter Harris, Jacob Eayrs, Billey Readhead, John Tompson, Joue, Pattrick Brown, George Cantey, Jacob Scott, Bobb, James Eayrs, Little Stephen, Little Charley, John Celliah, Petter George, George White, Jack Simmons, Billey Scott, Young John, Tom Cook." While Drennan requested pay for only 41 Catawba warriors, Draper remembered "at least 150" Indians had served under Sumter. Surely some of these were Cheraw,

A Wandering Tribe

Pee Dee, Saponi, Waccamaw or others who may not have so readily self-identified as "Catawba."

Sumter held his Native soldiers in high regard. One fellow veteran being entertained at the General's home remarked "The General is oft visited by the Catawba Indians who had served under him, many times arriving without notice." Several early historical accounts of Sumter County add to the record of these Catawba "scouts" by reflecting that Sumter had "invited some of his former scouts to live near him, and on his land" and indeed, the extent records show at least two Indian blooded men, David Scott and James Scott were among the few non-blood related persons to actually reside on the old General's estate.

Revolutionary War era "peace medal" gorget presented to Catawba Indian Piney George.

Major Catawba Out-Migrations

1830-1850

The rise of James Kegg to the leadership of the Catawba Nation in the late 1830's heralded the single largest mass exodus of Indians from the reservation. Kegg was, by even the most conservative accounts, opportunistic and anti-communal, and actively promoted the idea of abandoning the Catawba homeland for greener pastures in other areas. A description of Kegg's desires for the Catawba, as outlined in documents accompanying Governor Henagan's 1840 Report to the Legislature, are revealing:

"He wanted the title [to the new land set aside in North Carolina] in his own name and was willing the State where they settled, should Tax them, and make them subject to the Laws, and then they would be entitled to the privileges and immunities of citizens...General Kegg says, he wants to marry his women to the Cherokees, and then by the laws and customs of Indians, they would all become Catawbas, and in that way strengthen his tribe."

Kegg himself led a large contingent of Catawba to western North Carolina to live alongside the Cherokee remnants that remained there, and Kegg also personally signed the Treaty of Nation Ford in 1840 which relinquished 144,000 acres of Catawba land to the state of South Carolina.

The portion of the Catawba that had thrown their lot in with the Cherokee soon found the living conditions not to their liking. The Cherokee wanted these new Indian immigrants to "give up their tongue and nationality", something the majority of the Catawba could not stomach. To compound the injury, the state of South Carolina failed to complete negotiations with North Carolina to lay out reservation land for the Catawba, thus leaving them homeless once again.

A Wandering Tribe

When it became painfully obvious that South Carolina was not going to live up to their end of the Treaty of Nation Ford and secure a new reservation attached to the Cherokee, some of them, including James Kegg the very man who had pushed so hard for their move to the Cherokee, turned their faces to the east and began entreating the Palmetto State to allow their return. Others, under the leadership of William Morrison, petitioned the Office of Indian Affairs to secure funding to remove to Indian Territory.

In 1853 South Carolina Governor Seabrook ordered Indian Agent B.S. Massey to journey to the North Carolina Cherokee reservation and report back regarding the condition of the Catawba living there. Massey reported:

"After collecting them at the Cherokee Nation, I soon found that I could not unite and settle them with the Cherokee Indians. I then urged them to return to South Carolina…and they agreed to do so, and they soon commenced their return, and have continued to come in small parties up to this time."

Two years earlier, 22 of the Catawba living among the Cherokee had, at their own expense, immigrated to the Choctaw Nation in Indian Territory. The same year Indian Agent Massey was ordering the Catawba to return to South Carolina, 15 of that immigrant party of 22 were allowed to become citizens of the Choctaw Nation.

Indian agent Massey further reported in 1853 that another set of the Catawba had opted to neither stay near their old reservation, nor rely on the good graces of their ancient enemy the Cherokee:

"5 Catawbas have gone to Charleston, S.C. in 1851. One of them, General James Kegg died in Charleston in 1852 at the age of 69, the oldest member of the Tribe. Of the others, to wit Lewis Stephens, Jim

Major Catawba Out-Migrations

Morrison, a child and Polly Stephens, most or all still live in Charleston at this time, but have not been heard from since."

This group had taken up residence within a large community of Indian mixed-bloods who had established a settlement in St. Luke's and St. Paul's Parishes of Beaufort County, just north of the City of Charleston. This community, and the historical documentation of Indian ancestry for its citizens, is discussed in-depth as an addendum to this publication.

The majority of Catawba families who had left the area of the old reservation prior to 1850 broke off contact with the Indian Agent, most likely considering their rights and interest in the land to have been terminated with the 1840 Treaty, and never returned to their ancient river home.

Even before the disastrous Treaty of 1840, the Catawba were enduring a landless, nomadic lifestyle. Governor Henagan's 1840 Report to the Legislature describes them as:

"...for the past few years, they have been wandering through the country, forming a kind of Camps, without any homes, or fixed residence, and destitute of any species of property, save dogs, and a few worthless horses..."

Of the landless period of 1830 to 1850, no better description of the dispersal of the Catawba Nation can be given than by James Kegg, son of the man who had promoted the evacuation of the Catawba reservation:

Many years ago…the Catawba Indians, leased the land [we] owned in South Carolina and became a wandering tribe, without homes for [our] wives and children.

A Wandering Tribe

1880-1900

In 1883 Mormon missionaries ventured onto the Catawba reservation and found a large number of the Indians eager to convert to their brand of religion. The wave of Catawba out-migration during this era was a direct result of Mormon influence and resulted in several Catawba families uprooting for new lives in western areas such as Texas, Colorado, New Mexico, and Utah. The vast majority of these Indian converts maintained communication with their relatives on the old reservation, some preserving their "Catawba" identity to this day, and a few even returned to the Reservation within a generation or two.

> "My name is James Robbins and I am about 90 years of age. I was born in Orange County, NC. I came to Indiana in 1843. I know the family of Jerry Shocraft who has just testified. Silas Shocraft was my mother's brother. I think he was at least a ½ blood. At the time of my knowing old man Silas Shoecraft there were not many Cherokee Indians living in that section of NC and we did not know very much about them. There was no color blood in Silas Shocrafts family and one of them were ever held as slaves. I claim to be of Indian descent and did not apply to participate in this fund because I thought it was all a 'water haul.' My grandfather was named William Shocraft. He had no recognition as a Cherokee Indian because there were not many in that part of NC. My grandmother was named Bicey Nickens and she was supposed to be a full blood Cherokee Indian, and was an Indian doctor, and went around doctoring the women. There was no talk of Indians in that County. **I have heard of Catawba Indians being in that County.**"
> - August 13, 1908 testimony of James Robbins (born 1818) to support Cherokee Land Settlement claim of Jerry Shorcraft of Marion, Indiana.

FAMILY SKETCHES

CAUTION TO THE READER

One should not assume inclusion of any individuals or families within this publication 'proves' any descent from, or incontrovertible connection to, the historic Catawba Tribe, only that at some point an ancestor of that family group was described as a "Catawba" within an affidavit, newspaper article, legislative petition, etc. Within the historic period, tribal affiliations were often misquoted, mislabeled, or intentionally exaggerated for a host of reasons and readers should be cautioned against placing a great deal of weight on any one historic source.

BROWN

Rachel Brown Eady (born circa 1780 Catawba Reservation, SC) a full-blooded Catawba Indian, wife of George Eady of St Johns, SC.

1814:
Affidavit of Thomas Lee, Comptroller General of South Carolina:

> "Evidence being adduced to prove that Rachel Eady, wife of George Eady, was born of free Indian parents, neither she or her issue are liable for the poll tax."

27 Dec 1858:
Affidavit of Samuel Foxworth of Charleston SC:

> "Laura Breach is the granddaughter of George Eady, who was in all cases recognized as an Indian, and who did marry…Rachel Brown. And she, the said Laura Breech, is the descendant of the said George Eady and his wife Rachel, nee Brown."

29 Dec 1858:
Affidavit of Robert Austin of St. Johns Berkeley:

> "...he knows Laura Breech and her family formerly of the Parish of St. Johns Berkeley, now of the City of Charleston...they have always been regarded and treated as Free Indians."

James "Jamey" Brown (born circa 1790 Catawba Reservation, SC) was a full-blooded Catawba Indian, the son of Catawba leader Major John Brown. According to the Catawba reservation lease rent book,

> "Jamey Brown Catawba Indian intermarried with a Pamunkey Pocahontas." This would be Sally 'Sarah' Mursh, the daughter of Robert and Elizabeth Mursh. James "Jamey" Brown was dead by Sept 1820 as his widow, Sally began collecting his reservation lease rents.

One or more of Jamey and Sally Brown's children moved to Florida before 1820 as there is a notation within the Catawba reservation land lease rent books that directed a portion of his former lease payments be sent to "Quincy West Florida Apalachicola District."

The postal service of Quincy, Florida served all of Gadsden County. In 1855 the entire southern half of Gadsden County was carved off to form Liberty County.

1860 census Rescoe's Bluff, Liberty County, Florida:

Household # 132:

Brown, John........white.......male.......age: 40......born: SC
Brown, Emily.......white.......female....age: 35.......born: SC
Brown, Anderson...white.......male......age: 20......born: SC
Brown, Rebecca....white.......female....age: 16......born: SC
Brown, Sarah........white......female.....age: 13.......born: SC
Brown, Mary.........white......female....age: 11......born: SC
Brown, Emma........white.......female....age: 9.......born: SC

Brown

Brown, Elizabeth….white……female….age: 8…….born: SC
Brown, Dolly………white…....female….age: 3…….born: SC
Brown, Mahaly…….white…....female….age: 1…….born: SC
Brown, Lavina……..white……female….age: 1……born: SC

1870 census Bristol, Liberty County, Florida:

Household # 80:

Brown, Emily……white….female……age: 52…….born: Ga
Brown, Rebecca….white…female……age: 25…….born: FL
Brown, Sarahan…..white…female……age: 23…….born: FL
Brown, Tully……..white….male………age: 1……...born: FL
Brown, Emma……white….female……age: 16…….born: FL
Brown, Elizabeth…white…female……age: 15……..born: FL
Brown, Vina………white…female…….age: 12……born: FL
Brown, John………white….male……....age: 6……..born: FL

Sarah Brown (born circa 1760 SC) a full-blooded Catawba Indian. She married Thomas Gibbs, a descendant of the Appalachee Indians.

William "Billy" Brown (born 1729 York County, SC) was a ½ blooded Catawba Indian, son of Indian Trader Thomas Brown and a Catawba woman.

4 Dec 1745:
Will of Thomas Brown, York County, SC:

> Bequeathed two tracts of land totaling 361 acres to "…my natural son, born of a free Indian woman of the Catawba Nation…..my son, William Brown, aged 15 years…"

A Wandering Tribe

**Billie Kever Son of Mary Brown & Frank Kever
Liberty County, FL**

BUNCH

William Bunch (born circa 1710 SC) signed the 1759 petition of Catawba Indians.

Howard Bunch (born circa 1790 SC) married Philadelphia "Delphia" Marsh (born 1794), a Pamunkey Indian living on the Catawba Reservation.

James Bunch (born circa 1780 SC) was at least ¼ Indian, the grandson of Kesiah Breech, great-grandson of George Eady (a ½ blooded Indian of unknown tribal origin) and Rachel Brown (a full-blooded Catawba Indian).

7 Oct 1766:

Land Plat in Berkeley County, SC:

> "Pursuant to a precept from John Tramp Esq dated the 5th day of August 1766, I have admensured and laid out unto James Bunch a tract of land containing one hundred acres situated and being in Berkley County on a branch of the Four Holes Swamp known by the name of Target. Butting and bounded on all sides on vacant land."

16 June 1772:

Land Plat in St. Matthew's, Berkeley County, SC:

> "Pursuant to a precept from John Bremar esq dated the 2nd day of June 1772, I have admensured and laid out for Jacob Bunch a Tract of Two hundred acres of Landin St. Matthew's Berkley County, Bounding North West on John Bunch's Land, North East on William Bunch's Land, S.E. on James Bunch's land, and the other sides on vacant Land."

15

A Wandering Tribe

27 May 1799:

Affidavit of Matthew Winningham of St. John's Berkeley:

> "…he was well acquainted with the mother of James Bunch, who was the daughter of Kesiah Beech, whose mother he had frequently seen when he was a lad. [The Bunch paternal line]…were all esteemed as descendants of Egyptians who were all free people."[see affidavits regarding Beech/Breech family among EADY family below]

1850 census of St. Paul's Parish, Colleton County, SC:

Household # 51:

Bunch, Andrew R N….white……male……age: 38……..born: SC
Bunch, Elizabeth……..white……female….age: 38……..born: SC
Bunch, Joe…………….white…...male……age: 36……..born: SC
Bunch, Sarah…………..white…...female…age: 15……..born: SC
Bunch, Susan…………..white…..female….age: 11……..born: SC
Bunch, William………..white…..male…….age: 8………born: SC
Bunch, Henry………….white…...male…….age: 4……..born: SC
Stephens, Sarah………..white…...female….age: 50…….born: SC
Stephens, Sarah………..white…...female….age: 14……..born: SC
Stephens, Mary………...white…..female…..age: 90…….born: SC

1863:

Catawba Indians sent a petition to the SC Legislature regarding Agent J.R. Patton:

signor: Delphia Bunch

CANTY

Eliza Scott Canty (born 1826, Catawba Reservation, SC) was a full-blooded Catawba Indian the daughter of John Joe and Katy Scott Joe. Eliza Scott married Franklin Canty in 1843.

John Alonzo (Scott) Canty (born 9 Nov 1858, Catawba Reservation, SC) was a half-blood Catawba Indian, son of a white man, Thomas Whitesides, and Elizabeth Scott Canty. J Alonzo Canty first married Harriet Harris. Second he married Georgia Henrietta "Rhett" Patterson (born 4 July 1870) a half-blood Catawba Indian, daughter of James Patterson and Elizabeth White.

1880 census for York County, SC (included those residing on the Catawba Reservation):

Household # 288:

Canty, Lonzo…………..Indian…..male………age: 22…..born: SC
Canty, Harriet………..Indian…..female……..age: 23…..born: SC
Canty, Nettie H………Indian…..female….…..age: 7…….born: SC
Canty, William H…….Indian…..male………..age: 4…….born: SC
Canty, Lottie E………..Indian…..female……..age: 2…….born: SC
Canty, James J………..Indian…..male………age: 1…….born: SC

1900 census for Conejos, Sanford County, Colorado:

Household # 214:

Canty, Alonzo………white……male…….age: 41……born: SC
Canty, Georgia H…...white……female…..age: 29……born: SC
Canty, Williford M…white……male…….age: 7……..born: Colorado
Canty, Edward A……white……male……..age: 2……born: Colorado

A Wandering Tribe

1910 census for Conejos, Sanford County, Colorado (Special Indian Inquires Addendum):

Household #1:

Canty, J. Alonzo....Indian.....male....age: 57....born: SC...Catawba
Canty, Georgia K....Indian.....female..age: 39....born: SC...Catawba
Canty, Williford M.Indian.....male....age: 17....born: SC...Catawba
Canty, Eddie A......Indian.....male....age: 12....born: SC...Catawba
Canty, William F....Indian.....male....age: 8.....born: SC...Catawba
Canty, Zellia.........Indian.....male....age: 5.....born: SC...Catawba

1920 census for Conejos, Sanford County, Colorado:

Household # 60:

Canty, Wilford........Indian.....male......age: 26.....born: Colorado
Canty, Florence.......white.....female.....age: 39.....born: Utah
Christensen, Arneta...white.....female.....age: 73.....born: Norway
Christensen, Chase L.white.....male.......age: 30.....born: Colorado
Canty, Alonzo.........Indian....male......age: 61.....born: SC
Canty, Hanna E........Indian....female.....age: 49....born: SC
Canty, Eddie.........Indian.....male....age: 12.....born: Colorado
Canty, William......Indian.....male....age: 8.......born: Colorado
Canty, Lazell........Indian.....male....age: 5......born: Colorado

1930 census for Conejos, Sanford County, Colorado:

Household # 35:

Canty, Wilford......white.....male......age: 37.....born: Colorado
Canty, Florence......white.....female....age: 8......born: Colorado
Canty, Doris.........white.....female....age: 73.....born: Colorado

Household # 36:

Canty, Alonzo.........white....male......age: 71....born: SC

Canty, William F……white….male……age: 28….born: Colorado
Canty, Alma………..white…..male……age: 17….born: Colorado
Canty, Eddie A……..white…..male……age: 31….born: Colorado
Canty, Lena E……….white…..female….age: 27….born: Kansas

J Alonzo (Scott) Canty

CLARK

William Clark (born circa 1780) was at least ½ blooded Catawba Indian.

23 Mar 1807:
Affidavit of John Gough of St. Phillips, Charleston, SC:

> "…made oath that William Clark, William Ellis, and Charlotte Gill are descendants immediately from a native Indian woman born in this state in the parish of St. James, Goose Creek; and that the said three persons were also born in the said parish."

28 July 1807:
Affidavit of John Gough of St. Phillips, Charleston, SC:

> "…appeared and made oath that William Clark, Thomas Ellis and Charlotte Gill are descendants immediately from a native Indian woman of the Catawba nation, born in this state in the parish of St. Phillips, Charleston."

A Wandering Tribe

**Clark Indian family
Summerville, SC**

COLE

William "Old Billie" Cole (born circa 1770 North Carolina) was at least ½ Indian of unknown tribal origin. This Cole family appears to have origins in Buncombe County, North Carolina, and prior to that Lee County, Virginia. Old Billie and his wife immigrated into Floyd County, Kentucky circa 1830 and his progeny flourished there and spread into neighboring Magoffin County.

22 April 1889:
Article appearing in the Weekly Courier Journal entitled "A Tribe of Indians Which Continue to Flourish in Floyd County":

> "A woman with a very yellow face came to the door…informed us that she was Bet – the great-granddaughter of Old Bill Cole, the aged Cherokee Indian chief who had died on the same hill ten years before. Cole the head of a tribe of half-breeds about a hundred and fifty of his people still live on the same ridge. He was 110 years old when he died and his grave is on the highest spur of the mountain where his home still stands."

07 October 1901:
Article appearing in The Tennessean entitled "Kentucky's Indians – Old Billie Cole's Progeny":

> "It is not generally known that there are Indians scattered all over the mountains of Kentucky, but in nearly every county of the eastern section may be found one or more families named Cole, Perkins, Collins, Sizemore, Mullins, or Nickels, many of whom are in some way related to "Old Billie" Cole, a Catawba Chief, who came here from North Carolina and settled in Floyd County nearly a century ago.
> The greatest number of "old Billie's" descendants living in one place is the Cole family in Big Lick Branch, in Magoffin County. The correspondent recently visited the "Cole Nation," as it is called up there, and had a long interview with "Chief Tiney."…When seen by the correspondent "Uncle Tiney," as everybody calls him, was sitting on the porch giving orders to

some boys who were repairing a rail fence near the house. He was bareheaded, and his primitive clothes and his long hair made him look like the typical planter and Indian...In response to questions, Chief Tiney gave the following narrative: "I was bred and born in Kentucky, but I don't know just where. Before I came to the Big Lick I lived at different places in Breathitt, Floyd, Johnson and Lawrence counties. My father, 'Old Billie' Cole, came from North Carolina. He was three-quarters Indian and was not allowed to vote until after the war, but I voted ever since I was 21 years old...I don't know much about my people. 'Old Billie,' my father, brought my mother from Virginia. He had two wives and nine children. He was 106 years old when he died here on Big Lick."

November 1950:

Entry in the Ohio Journal of Science by Edward T. Price entitled "The Mixed-Blood Racial Strain of Carmel, Ohio, and Magoffin County, Kentucky":

> "The mixed-bloods are accepted without question as to origin or status...They are usually considered to be part Indian, though a few people prefer to call it Negro...Their habits of ridge farming and of hunting with their numerous dogs are usually attributed to their Indian blood...There are, perhaps 200 of the mixed-bloods in Magoffin County now; they are considered to be fewer in number and less Indian-like in appearance than in the earlier days recalled by old-timers...This area was dominated by the Cole family and it is yet known as the "Cole Nation.""

1860 census of Magoffin County, KY:

Household # 26:

Cole, Charles.........Indian....male......born: 1826...born: KY
Cole, Charlotte.......Indian....female....born: 1826....born: KY
Cole, Wallace.........Indian.....male......born: 1848...born: KY
Cole, Shepard.........Indian.....male......born: 1849....born: KY

Cole

Cole, Apperson…….Indian…..male……born: 1851…born: KY
Cole, Nancy………...Indian….female….born: 1854…born: KY
Cole, Pego…………..Indian….female….born: 1858…born: KY

Household # 502:

Cole, Valentine……Indian……male……born: 1812…..born: KY
Cole, Mariah……….Indian…...female….born: 1812…..born: KY
Cole, Parline……….Indian……female…born: 1824…..born: KY
Cole, George……….Indian……male……born: 1847….born: KY
Cole, Adam………...Indian……male……born: 1851….born: KY
Cole, Rufus…………Indian……male……born: 1854….born: KY

Household # 507:

Cole, John……….Indian…….male……born: 1837……born: KY
Cole, Nancy……..Indian……female….born: 1837……born: KY
Cole, Dicey……...Indian……female….born: 1854……born: KY
Cole, Jensey……..Indian……female….born: 1857……born: KY
Cole, Jesse……….Indian……male……born: 1859……born: KY

1880 census of Magoffin County, KY:

Household # 201:

Cole, Tiney [Sr]…Indian……male…...born: 1786……born: NC
Cole, Mariah……Indian……female…born: 1794……born: VA
Cole, Nancy…….Indian……female…born: 1835..d-n-law..born: KY
Cole, Jefferson….Indian……male…...born: 1853.step-son…born: KY
Cole, Narcissus….Indian….....male…..born: 1853.son…born: KY

Household # 202:

Cole, Adam……..Indian…….male……born: 1830…born: KY
Cole, Christina…Indian…….female….born: 1833…born: KY

Household # 203:

Cole, Tiney [Jr]…..Indian…male…….born: 1831…born: KY

25

A Wandering Tribe

Cole, Sara J..........Indian...female.....born: 1834...born: KY

Household # 204:

Cole, John W.......Indian......male......born: 1831...born: KY
Cole, Rebecca......Indian......female....born: 1837...born: KY

Household # 251:

Cole, Lotta.....Indian......female...born: 1810...widow...born: KY
Cole, Calvin...Indian......male......born: 1843..............born: KY
Cole, Louisa...Indian......female....born: 1846.............born: KY
Cole, Page......Indian.......male......born: 1847.............born: KY
Cole, Sarah.....Indian......female....born: 1831.............born: KY

Household # 206:

Cole, Meredith..Indian......male......born: 1836......born: KY
Cole, Wemily....Indian......female...born: 1835.......born: KY
Cole, Lara........Indian......female...born: 1849......born: KY
Little, Lealey..Indian....male..born: 1855...step-son...born: KY

Household # 207:

Cole, Amanda....Indian...female....born: 1836.unmarried...born: KY
Cole, Nelson......Indian......male......born: 1854.........born: KY
Cole, Tennessee...Indian......male......born: 1859.........born: KY

Household # 208:

Cole, George...Indian......male.......born: 1811......born: KY
Cole, Nancy.....Indian......female.....born: 1812......born: KY
Cole, Jalaza.....Indian......female.....born: 1846......born: KY
Cole, Survilla...Indian......female.....born: 1849......born: KY
Cole, Monk......Indian......male......born: 1852.......born: KY
Cole, William [Old Billie].Indian.male.born: 1780.father.born: NC
Cole, Rebecca..Indian......female...born: 1810..step-mother...b: KY
Cole. George...Indian....male.....born: 1849..neph...born: KY
Cole, Ollivia...Indian...female...born: 1853..niece..born: KY

Cole

Stewart, Wilie..Indian...male...born: 1880..grand-son..born: KY

Household # 211:

Cole, Fereby...Indian...female.....born: 1827...widow..born: KY
Cole, Mary......Indian....female.....born: 1842...born: KY
Cole, Lereta.....Indian....female....born: 1844....born: KY
Cole, Malenda..Indian....female....born: 1850...born: KY
Cole, Lotta......Indian....female....born: 1848....born: KY

Household # 213:

Cole, John......Indian......male......born: 1811......born: KY
Cole, Jancy J...Indian......female....born: 1814......born: KY
Cole, Lonzo.....Indian......male.......born: 1842......born: KY
Cole, Rosena....Indian......female...born: 1851......born: KY
Cole, Daniel.....Indian......male......born: 1845......born: KY
Cole, Martha....Indian......female....born: 1854......born: KY
Cole, Margaret..Indian......female....born: 1847......born: KY
Cole, Susan......Indian......female...born: 1856.......born: KY

Household # 214:

Cole, Jesse......Indian....male........born: 1840......born: KY
Cole, Jane......Indian.....female......born: 1846......born: KY

1900 Special Indian census of Magoffin County, KY:

Cole, Fereby.......Indian....female......born: 1835....born: KY
Cole, Sereta........Indian....female......born: 1864....born: KY
Cole, Lota..........Indian....female......born: 1868....born: KY
Cole, Malinda......Indian....female......born: 1872....born: KY
Cole, Violet..Indian..female..born: 1886..grand-dau...born: KY
Cole, Jesse...Indian..male....born: 1897..grand-son...born: KY

Nickels, John..Indian...male....born: 1863...widower..born: KY
Cole, Dicey...Indian...female..born: 1867....servant...born: KY
Cole, Don......Indian...male....born: 1895...lodger....born: KY
Cole, Page.....Indian...male....born: 1857.........born: KY

A Wandering Tribe

Cole, Artsy....Indian...female..born: 1872.........born: KY

Cole, John W...Indian...male.......born: 1862........born: KY
Cole, Rebecca...Indian...female.....born: 1862........born: KY
Cole, Narcissus.Indian...female.....born: 1882........born: KY
Cole, Garrett....Indian....male......born: 1883........born: KY
Cole, Wiley......Indian....male......born: 1885........born: KY
Cole, Morgan....Indian....male......born: 1889........born: KY
Cole, Birdine.....Indian....male......born: 1891........born: KY
Cole, Louisa......Indian....female....born: 1893........born: KY
Cole, Izana.......Indian....female.....born: 1895.......born: KY
Cole, Mangun...Indian....male.......born: 1897........born: KY
Cole, Silvester...Indian....male.......born: 1880........born: KY
Cole, Lula.........Indian...female.....born: 1882........born: KY
Cole, Jesse........Indian...male.......born: 1858........born: KY
Cole, Jane.........Indian...female.....born: 1861........born: KY
Cole, Preston.....Indian....male.......born: 1884.......born: KY
Cole, Isaac........Indian....male.......born: 1886.......born: KY
Cole, Martha.....Indian....female.....born: 1890.......born: KY
Cole, Anne........Indian...female.....born: 1893.......born: KY
Cole, Andrew.....Indian....male.......born: 1895.......born: KY
Cole, Zana.........Indian...female.....born: 1898.......born: KY
Cole, Nancy...Indian.....female......born:1837...mother.born: KY
Cole, Tiney [Jr]..Indian..female......born: 1858............born: KY
Cole, Sarah.......Indian..female......born: 1860.............born: KY
Cole, Adam......Indian....male......born: 1883...........born: KY
Cole, Clara...Indian..female....born: 1884..daug-in-law...born: KY

Cole

Daniel and Jahaza Cole

Alonzo Cole and Jona Gibson Cole

A Wandering Tribe

Preston Cole family

Hayes Charles Cole

EADY

The Eady surname is one of known Indian derivative in most areas it occurs in South Carolina. The majority of the Eady Indian family settled their own town, aptly named Eadytown, in what was to become Berkeley County. Frederick Porcher described Eadytown in 1881 as "a village of halfbreeds." In that same area, just north of Charleston, can be found numerous historical affidavits and Court filings regarding the Indian ancestry of the Eady family.

George Eady (born circa 1752) was at least ½ Indian of unknown tribal origin. George married Sarah Brown, a full-blooded Catawba Indian.

10 Feb 1824:
Affidavit of Benjamin Reynolds of St. Johns Island, Colleton County, SC:
"I hereby certify that the bearer George Eady is of the family of Mary Beamer, and that the said Mary descended from one of the tribe of Indians in amity with the white."

27 Dec 1858:
Affidavit of Samuel Foxworth of Charleston SC:
"Laura Breach is the granddaughter of George Eady, who was in all cases recognized as an Indian, and who did marry…Rachel Brown. And she, the said Laura Breech, is the descendant of the said George Eady and his wife Rachel, nee Brown."

Susannah Eady (born circa 1748)

31 May 1815:
Will of Susannah Eady of St. Johns Parish:
"…to be buried at my brother Daniel Eady's place." Also names a brother, George Eady, a sister, Mary Eady, two nieces, Nancy Eady and Peggy Eady, and one nephew, Jonathan Eady.

A Wandering Tribe

Daniel Eady (born circa 1750) was at least ½ Indian of unknown tribal origin. Daniel married Jemima, "daughter of Indian Sarah", a full-blooded Catawba Indian.

10 Sept 1834:
Will of Daniel Eady of St. Johns Parish:
"Daniel Eady, a fee coloured man of St. Johns Berkeley...to my daughter Esther Bluit, all my plantation, to her also my negro woman Nancy and all other negroes." Also names a granddaughter, Elizabeth Peigler and one nephew, Jonathan Eady.

Daniel Eady   **Jemima (daughter of Indian Sarah, full-blooded Catawba)**

Children:
- Esther Bluit Eady - married a white man, Lewis, then married a white man, Roberts
- Children (by Lewis): Eliza Lewis – married a white man, Jacob Edwards
  Children (by Roberts): Elizabeth Roberts – married a white man, Henry Peigler

Elizabeth (Eady) Roberts Peigler (born circa 1790 SC) was at least 3/4 Indian of mixed Catawba descent.

Henry P Peigler (white man)   **Elizabeth (Eady) Roberts**
Children:
- Rosana Peigler (born 1812)
- Robert Peigler (born 1816)
- Daniel Peigler (born 1817)
- James Peigler (born 1820)
- Elizabeth Peigler (born 1832)

1 Mar 1840:
Affidavit of Elizabeth Ann Bartlett of St. Johns Berkeley:

"...swears that she has known Elizabeth Peagler, the wife of Henry P. Peagler, ever since the said Elizabeth was a child. Deponent has always heard her own mother say that the same Elizabeth Peagler, formerly Roberts, was the descendant of an Indian woman of the Catawba Nation by the name of Hester Blute who intermarried with a white settler of the neighborhood by the name of Roberts, an Irishman, of which marriage the same Elizabeth was the offspring."

1 June 1840:
Affidavit of Eliza Ann Bartlett of St. Johns Berkeley:

"...swears that she has known Eliza Edwards the bearer of this certificate ever since her childhood...she is the offspring of Hester Blute, an Indian woman of the Catawba Tribe, by a Portuguese."

1 June 1840:
Affidavit of Catherine Burns of St. Stephens Parish, SC:

"...swears that she has known Eliza Edwards the bearer of this certificate ever since her childhood...she was intimately acquainted with the mother Hester Blute who was the daughter of Jemima who was the offspring of Indian Sarah...The whole of this family were of the Catawba Tribe."

A Wandering Tribe

**Robert Eady & Ida Bennett
Berkeley, SC**

EVANS

John Evans (born circa 1726 Congaree Fort, SC) was a ½ blooded Catawba Indian, the son of Indian Trader John Evans and a Catawba woman.

Sam Evans (born circa 1800 Catawba Reservation, SC) was a Catawba Indian who appeared twice in the Reservation Lease book circa 1827, but disappeared from the record after that.

Sarah (Evans) Canty Head (born 1 July 1845 Catawba Reservation, SC) was a full-blooded Catawba, daughter of Chancy Evans and Peggy Canty, and widow of Robert Henry Head.

Leven Evans (born circa 1775 Halifax, NC) was at least ½ Indian of unknown tribal origin. He married Harriet "Kizzie" Scott who was also at least ½ Indian of unknown tribal origin.

Leven Evans   **Harriet "Kizzie" Scott**
(born circa 1800/died 1841-1849)   (born circa 1810/ died after 1880)
Both lived and died in Halifax County, NC.
Children:
- William Evans (b 1835)
- Harriet Evans (b 1836)
- Dock Evans
- **Elijah Evans** (b 1846)   -m- (1st) **Jane C. Richardson**
  Children:
  - Thomas Henry Evans (b 1867)
  - Lucy Evans (b 1869)
  - Aleck Evans (b 1873)
  - Betsy Evans (b 1875)
  - Hayes Evans (b 1877)
  - Major Blake Evans (b 1879)
  - Fox Evans (b 1881)
              -m- (2nd) **Roxanna McGee**
  Children:
  - Lijah B Evans (b 1887)
  - Estella Evans (b 1891)

- Lizzie Evans (b 1893)
- Amos Evans (b 1894)
- Minnie Evans (b 1897)

-m- (3rd) **Rebecca J. Richardson**

Children:
- Dock Evans (b 1900)
- Karon Evans (b 1902)
- Elijah Evans (b 1904)
- William K Evans (b 1910)

August 1896:
Affidavits of Nick Shearin, John H Shearin, William Stokes, and James J King of Halifax, NC:
"The undersigned parties being duly sworn according to law, says and each for himself says, that he was well acquainted with Mariah Evans who was a daughter of Levans Evans and his wife Kizzie Evans; that the said Leven Evans & his wife Kizzie were full blooded Cherokee Indians and that Lucy Evans is the daughter of the said Mariah Evans; said Lucy Evans married Wm. Evans and has several children by said marriage. Affiants are in no way interested in said matter. The affiant Nick Shearin is 70 years old. The affiant John H. Shearin is 60 years old. The affiant Wm. Stokes is 81 years old and the affiant James J. King is 95 years old and all are residents of the community wherein said Evanses lived."

August 1896:
Affidavit of James J King of Halifax, NC:
"…states that he is a resident of Halifax County and are 95 years of age and that he is well acquainted with the ancestors of Elijah and Dock Evans, that his grandmother Peggy Scott was an Indian and his grandfather John Scott had Indian blood in him and they were the mother and father of Leven Evans and Harriet Evans who was the mother and father of Elijah and Dock Evans."

August 1896:
Affidavit of William Stokes of Halifax, NC:
"…that he is a resident of Halifax County and that he is 81 years of age and that he is personally acquainted with Elijah Evins and Dock Evins and their ancestors Leven Evins and Harriet Evins their father

Evans

and mother and John Scott and Peggy Scott their Grandfather, and mother. John Scott was the father of Harriet Evens and Peggy Scott was her mother and Elijah and Dock Evens is the sons of Harriet Evens and the grandsons of John Scott who was said to have Indian blood in him, and Peggy Scott was the grandmother of the said Elijah and Dock Evins and the said Peggy Scott was an Indian of the Cherokee Tribe."

26 Sept 1896:
In the matter of application of Solomon Evans, et. al., Cherokee Nation's No. 3108, Filed September 26, 1896, Louisburg, North Carolina "W.K.A. Williams being duly sworn according to law says that on Sept. 2, 1896 he saw a package registered at the P. O. at Louisburg, N.C. address to Hon. S. H. Mayes Tahlequah Ind. Ter. (Chief of Cherokee Tribe), that registry receipt No. 43 as received from the Post Master all attached is a receipt for and package which contains copies of the applications of Elijah Evans, Elijah Evans Jr., Thos. Henry Evans, Wm Evans, Lucy Evans, & Solomon Evans and of the affidavits of Nick Shearin, J. H. Shearin, Wm Stokes & James J. King in support of same."

2 Sept 1896:
Affidavit of Elijah Evans sworn to before Thomas B. Wilder:
"To the Honorable the Dawes Commission on Citizenship in the Five Civilized Tribes in the Indian Territory: Your petitioner Elijah Evans the undersigned respectfully states that he is a Cherokee Indian by blood and ask to be enrolled as a member of the Cherokee Nation of Indians in the Indian Territory.
That he derives his Indian blood from Leven Evans his father, who was Cherokee Indian by blood of at least be half blood. My age is 53 years. My Post Office address is Louisburg, NC. My family consists of my wife Roxanna and the following children: Thos. aged 30, Joseph aged 27, Lucy aged 25, Aleck aged 24, Betsy aged 22, Hayes aged 19, Major Blake aged 17, Fox aged 15, Lijah aged 8, Estella aged 6, Lizzie aged 4, Amos aged 1."

26 Aug 1896:
In the matter of application of SOLOMON EVANS, et. al., Nation's No. 3108 for citizenship in the Cherokee Nation, Before the Honora-

bles, Henry L. Dawes, Frank C. Armstrong, A. S. McKennon, T.B. Cabaniss, and A. B. Montgomery, Commissioners:
"Your respondent, S. H. Mayes, Principal Chief of the Cherokee Nation, comes now and demurs the said application, and for the grounds thereof says: 1st. That this Commission has not jurisdiction over the parties or subject matter of this controversy, and no legal right, therefore, to hear and determine the same. 2nd. That the application does not state facts sufficient, if true, to show the applicants are entitled to citizenship. Respondent not waiving his aforesaid demurrer, but insisting upon the same for answer to said application, says that Level Evans, through whom the petitioners claim to derive their right to citizenship in the Cherokee Nation, is not now, and has not been a citizen of the Cherokee Nation, since the removal of said Nation, west to the Indian Territory as at present located and defined; that his name does not appear on any of the authenticated rolls of said Nation; that neither he nor any of his ancestors now reside, or ever have resided in the Cherokee Nation and Indian Territory, as citizens thereof. Having fully answered, your respondent asks to be hence dismissed. S. H. Mayes, Principal Chief Cherokee Nation."

27 Sept 1896:
Case of Solomon Evans, et. al., Louisburg, NC
"Cherokee Nation, Filed Sept. 27, 1896. Rejected."

1860 census of Western District, Halifax County, NC:

Household # 587:

Evans, Harriett………..mulatto….female…..age: 49………born: NC
Evans, William………..mulatto….male…..age: 25…….born: NC
Evans, Harriett………..mulatto….female...age: 24……..born: NC
Evans, Elijah………….mulatto….male…..age: 14……..born: NC

1870 census of Washington Township, Nash County, NC:

Household # 309:

Scott, Elijah………mulatto….male……..age: 23………born: NC
Scott, Jane………...mulatto….female…..age: 25………born: NC

Evans

Scott, Thomas.......mulatto....male.........age: 3.........born: NC
Scott, Joana..........mulatto....female.....age: 1..........born: NC

1880 census of Brinkleyville, Halifax County, NC:

Household # 150:

Evans, Elijah.........mulatto....male........age: 33.........born: NC
Evans, Jane...........mulatto....female.....age: 29.........born: NC
Evans, Thomas.......mulatto....male........age: 12.........born: NC
Evans, Josephina.....mulatto....female......age: 11.........born: NC
Evans, Lucy A........mulatto....female......age: 10.........born: NC
Evans, Alex...........mulatto....male.........age: 8.........born: NC
Evans, Bettie.........mulatto....female.......age: 6.........born: NC
Evans, Hayes.........mulatto....male.........age: 3.........born: NC
Evans, Major Blake..mulatto....male.........age: 1.........born: NC
Evans, Harriet........mulatto....female......age:69.........born: NC

1900 census of Brinkleyville, Halifax County, NC:

Household # 70:

Evans, Elijah......black....male........age: 55.........born: NC
Evans, Major B....black....male........age: 20.......born: NC
Evans, Fox.........black....male........age: 18.......born: NC
Evans, Elijah Jr....black....male........age: 11.......born: NC
Evans, Stella.......black....female.....age: 10.........born: NC
Evans, Lizzie.......black....female......age: 7.........born: NC
Evans, Amos........black....male..........age: 5........born: NC
Evans, Minnie......black....female......age: 3.........born: NC
Evans, Adelene V..black....female......age: 24........born: NC

A Wandering Tribe

**John Evans 1830-1892
& wife Martha Harris**

Evans

Ira Evans
1879-1968

A Wandering Tribe

**Fox Evans
1882-1932**

Evans

Major B Evans
1879-1959

A Wandering Tribe

**Children of Major B Evans
Halifax, NC**

FLOWERS

Ben Flowers a.k.a. Long Ben (born circa 1737) was a mixed-blood Indian of unknown ancestry. Simon was the son of Tom and Betty Flowers and brother of Simon and Will Flowers.

Simon Flowers (born 1730 SC) was a mixed-blood Indian of unknown ancestry. Simon was the son of Tom and Betty Flowers and brother of Ben and Will Flowers.

Will Flowers (born circa 1735) was a mixed-blood Indian of unknown ancestry. Simon was the son of Tom and Betty Flowers and brother of Ben and Simon Flowers.

October 26, 1766:
> "Arrested: An Indian or Mustee fellow about 36 years of age, named Simon Flowers, has a small beard, and born at Santee, says he is free, but has nothing to prove it, that his father and mother were Indians, named Tom and Betty Flowers, his father dead, but his mother alive, has two brothers named Ben and Will, they all live on Santee. He says that when he was little his father bound him to one John Thomas, who lives six miles over the Santee River, near John Morrice and Stephen Willes, planters, and that all his relations live close by; he says his master has used him very ill, and would not let him go when his time was out, but intended to keep him as slave. He is marked on the right cheek, W, on his left with a single stroke thus, I, which he says his father did to all his children when they were small with a needle and gunpowder."

A Wandering Tribe

William E Gentry

GENTRY

Circa 1930:
Interview of Mrs. Caroline Everett, Oklahoma Indian Pioneer Interviews, Volume 28:

> "William E. Gentry was born in Calhoun County, Mississippi March 11, 1842, a son of James and Caroline Gentry…By ancestry he was a Catawba Indian adopted into the Creek tribe."

31 June 1937:
Interview of Willie Lerblance, Oklahoma Indian Pioneer Interviews, Volume 53:

> "My grandfather was Elija Hermigine Lerblance (La Blanche). He was born in March 1836, son of a Louisiana Frenchman, and Vicey Gentry, who was the daughter of Elijah Gentry (Colonel E.W. Gentry), a white who married a full-blood Catawba Indian. He came from Alabama to the Creek Nation with his parents at the age of 12 years (came into Indian Territory in approx. 1848)."

1850 census of Chickasaw County, Mississippi:
Household # 276:
Gentry, James G.….white….male……age: 36….born: Alabama
Gentry, Caroline….white….female….age: 38.....born: South Carolina
Gentry, Mary E.…...white….female….age: 11…born: Alabama
Gentry, William E...white….male…....age: 8.….born: Mississippi
Gentry, Levi L.…….white….male….…age: 6…born: Mississippi
Gentry, Albert J.…...white….male….…age: 3…born: Mississippi
Gentry, Nancy C.….white….female…..age: 1….born: Mississippi

1899:
Roll of Creek and Seminole by Blood, Indian Territory:

Roll # 1653:

A Wandering Tribe

Gentry, William E………..age: 57……….male…………...blood: 1/4
Gentry, Sallie D…………...age: 39……….female………..blood: 1/2
Gentry, Caroline……..…..age: 17……….female………..blood: 3/8
Gentry, Mary E…………...age: 15……….female………..blood: 3/8
Gentry, Sallie P…………..age: 13……….female………..blood: 3/8
Gentry, Robert L……..…..age: 11……….male…………..blood: 3/8
Gentry, Bluford M…..…...age: 9…….…..male…………..blood: 3/8
Gentry, Rachel J…………age: 7……...…female………..blood: 3/8
Gentry, Boyd E…………...age: 5…….…..male…………..blood: 3/8

1900 Special Indian census of Creek Nation, Indian Territory:

Household # 165:

Gentry, William…mixed…male……age: 58….born: Miss
Gentry, Sallie……mixed…female….age: 40….born: Indian Territory
Gentry, Caroline…mixed…female…age: 19….born: Indian Territory
Gentry, Mary…….mixed…female…age: 17….born: Indian Territory
Gentry, Sallie……mixed….female…age: 15….born: Indian Territory
Gentry, Robert…..mixed….male…...age: 12…..born: Indian Territory
Gentry, Bluford….mixed….male…...age: 10….born: Indian Territory
Gentry, Rachel…..mixed….female…age: 8…..born: Indian Territory
Gentry, Boyd…….mixed….male……age: 5….born: Indian Territory
Lerblanch, Andrew…mixed…male...age: 15….born: Indian Territory
Lerblanch, William…mixed....male...age: 13….born: Indian Territory
Lerblanch, Howard….mixed…male...age: 15…born: Indian Territory

GIBBS

3 Oct 1782:
Affidavit of Nathaniel Bullen of Charleston, SC:

> "…maketh oath that the mother of a certain mulatto, or tawny woman who is present in Charles Town, known by the name of Catherine Gibbes, was born free, being an Indian woman belonging to the Nation of Indians called the Appulatche."

Levicey "Vicey" Gibbs (born circa 1798 SC) daughter of Thomas Gibbs, a descendant of the Appalachee Indians, and Sarah Brown, a Catawba Indian. Vicey Gibbs Goins lived to be at least 90 years old, managed to retain a major portion of her father's original land holdings, and was an invaluable informant to Sumter County historian McDonald Furman.

1888:
"Old Timers" article, Jackson, Mississippi newspaper:
"Vicey Goins, and 'old time' free woman of Privateer, S. C., recently died. She was thought to be 90 years old. Her husband was the son of an Indian woman, who was a fortune teller. At one time she owned about 350 acres of land."

A Wandering Tribe

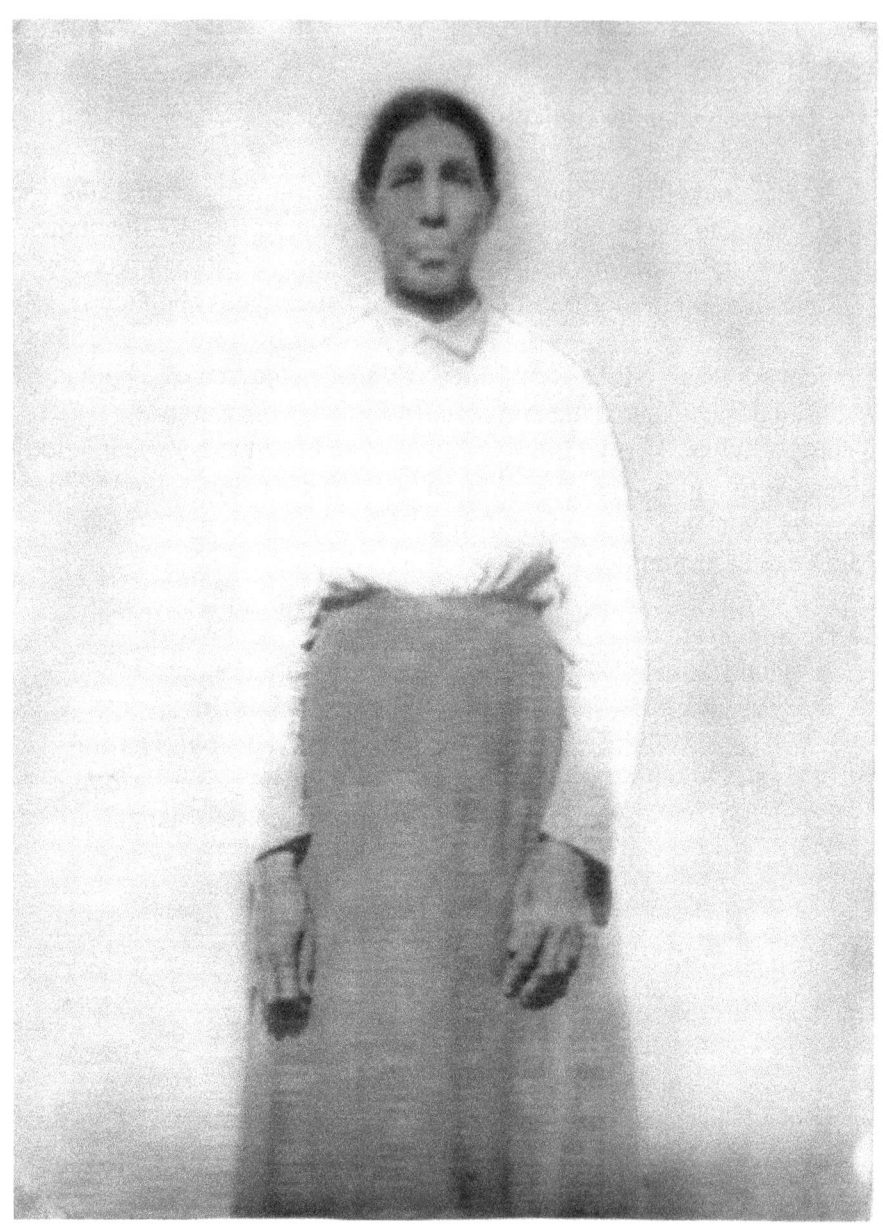

Levicey 'Vicey' Gibbs Goins

GOINS/GOINGS

Jeremiah Goins (born: before 1780 Berkeley, SC, died before 1830 Sumter, SC) was at least ¼ Indian of unknown tribal origin. Jeremiah was the son of Frederick Goins (who died in service at the Siege of Charleston in 1780) and Mary Burbage. Jeremiah married Eady Lucas, who was at least ½ Catawba Indian.

Thomas Goins (born circa 1800 SC) was the son of Jeremiah Goins and Eady Lucas. Thomas married Levicey 'Vicey' Gibbs, who was at least ½ Catawba Indian.

Aug 1893:
Interview of Rebecca Jacobs by McDonald Furman, Sumter, SC: "…[Eady Lucas Goins] said she came from the Catawba tribe."

Thomas Goins   Levicy 'Vicey' Gibbs

Children:
- Thomas Goins (born 1819) married Martha 'Mahala' Chavis
- Matilda Goins (born 1820) married James E Smiling
- Mary 'Polly' Goins (born 1821) married James Gibbs
- Lavincey 'Vincy' Goins (born 1822) married Lysender 'Lon' Benenhaley
- John Goins (born 1822) married Jane Winkles
- Thomas Goins Jr (born 1823)
- Wade Goins (born 1824) married Abigail Avon
- Madrid 'Madry' Goins (born 1827) married Lavicey Tucker

March 24, 1860:

Article appearing in The Greensboro Times, Stokes County, North Carolina:

> "On Wednesday there was a case which excited considerable interest, the case of the State vs. **Enoch Going**. The State was represented by Mr. Solicitor Masten, and Going was defended by J.R. McLean and A.H. Joyce, Esquires. This was an in-

dictment against the said defendant, who was charged in the bill as being a free negro, for migrating into this State from Virginia, contrary to our Act of Assembly. The defendant, through his counsel, denied that he is a free negro, and alleged that he is of Indian extraction. The Jury, on the testimony before them, acquitted him."

Matilda Goins (born 1820 Sumter, SC) was the daughter of Thomas Goins and Levicey 'Vicey' Gibbs. McDonald Furman wrote of her,

> "an old woman of about 71 years, and is considerably mixed with Indian: her face is not unlike one of that race."

Wade Goins (born 1824 Sumter, SC) was the son of Thomas Goins and Levicey 'Vicey' Gibbs. McDonald Furman wrote of him,

> "…Wade Goins is one of the old people among the Privateer Redbones and his features and copper-colored skin show the presence of Indian blood in his veins."

Goins/Goings

Rena K Goins
Daughter of Madrid Goins and Levicey Tucker
Sumter, SC

A Wandering Tribe

1888:
"Recollections of Seventy Years" by Payne, Daniel Alexander (1811-1893):

> "I was born of free parents in the city of Charleston, SC, on the 24th of Feb. 1811…As far as memory serves me my mother was of light-brown complexion…she told me that her grandmother was of a tribe of Indians known in the early history of the Carolinas as the Catawba Indians. The husband of her grandmother was a black man named Alexander Goings, who was remarkable for great bodily strength and activity."

GORDON

Isaac "Stell" Gordon (born 1836 Beaufort District Indian Settlement) was at least ½ Indian of unknown tribal origin, son of David Gordon and Eliza Bing (the daughter of Betsy Busby). He was a blacksmith's apprentice to David Billings of Lancaster in 1860. He married Lucinda Harris, a full-blooded Catawba Indian.

Lewis Harris Gordon (born August 1869 Fort Mill, SC) was ½ Catawba Indian the son of Isaac "Stell" Gordon and Lucinda Harris. He married Sallie Brown, a full-blooded Catawba, daughter of John Brown and Margaret George.

1900 Special Indian census, Catawba Reservation, York County, SC:

Household # 14:

Gordan, Lewis……………………..Indian…..male………..age: 30
Gordan, Sallie…………………...Indian…..female……age: 33
Gordan, Nora…………………....Indian…..female……age: 15
Gordan, Rhett…………………..Indian…..female……age: 2
Harris, William………………...Indian…..male………..age: 44
Harris, Butler…………………..Indian…..male………..age: 22
Harris, David…………………...Indian…..male………..age: 24
Gordan, Lilly Irwin…………...Indian…..female……age: 1

Nan Gordon married Tom Harris, a full-blooded Catawba Indian.

A Wandering Tribe

**Sallie Brown Gordon
Wife of Lewis Gordon**

GUY

William Guy (born circa 1760 Brunswick County, VA, died 20 Jan 1836 Granville, NC) was at least ½ Catawba Indian. William Guy married Abigail Chavers 10 Jan 1780 in Granville, NC. William served in Captain Vaughn's Mecklenburg Company of Virginia Colonial Militia in the Revolutionary War. He filed for his veteran's pension 5 Feb 1833 in Granville County, NC.

William Guy   **Abigail Chavers**
Children:
- Vines Guy (born: 1785) married Elizabeth Jeffries
- Buckner Guy (born: 1793) married Sylvia Jeffries
- John Guy (born: 1792) married Aggy Whitmore
- Richard Guy (born: 1794) married Martha Whitmore
- Edmond Guy (born: 1798) married Judith Jeffries
- Jesse Guy (born: 1800)
- Henry Guy (born: 1805)
- James Guy (born 1810)

In the 1820's, three of William Guy's sons, Buckner Guy, Richard Guy, and John Guy, moved south to Macon County to settle land newly ceded by the Cherokee Nation.

Oct 1869:
Letter from Dr. Joseph McDowell to Eli Parker, U.S. Commissioner of Indian Affairs:

> "I take the Liberty of addressing to you a few lines on behalf of a remnant of the tribe of Catawba Indians…Some 60 or 70 years since they left their tribe and went to Greenville County, Virginia, and then removed to Orange County, North Carolina…they sold out in Orange and moved to Macon County, N.C. where they purchased land and remained every since."

Oct 1872:
U.S. Senate Document #144, entitled "The Catawba Tribe of Indians":

A Wandering Tribe

"Dr. Joseph McDowell, of Fairmont, GA, asking relief of the Government…Catawba Indians, and 81 in number…wishing the government to assist them in moving west to Indian Territory…William Guy, of Granville County, Ga (sic NC), and Simon Jeffries, of Bellville, Virginia, Catawba Indians, served five years in the Army and were honorably discharged, and these people are their descendants."

March 28, 1896:
Letter of Department of the Interior, Office of Indian Affairs, Washington, DC:

"No action appears to have been taken by the government or any of the [Catawba] Indians on the question of their removal to the Choctaw or other Indian country until 1872, when Hon H. C. Harper, of the House of Representatives from Georgia, brought to the attention of this office the question of the removal of certain Indians from North Carolina and Georgia. Presuming they were Cherokees, this office requested him on the 13th of June, 1872, to furnish a list of the names and ages of said Indians. In reporting the names, Mr. Joseph McDowell of Fairmont, Georgia, under date of October 1872 (Misc. M., 229) stated that the Indians referred to, and asking relief of the government, were Catawba Indians, and 84 in number.

1. Buckner Guy…………………………….age: 80
2. Lucinda Anderson, his daughter, wife of Wm Anderson, a Cherokee…………………………….age: 60
3. Polly Guy…………………………….age: 50
4. James Guy…………………………….age: 55
5. Clark Guy…………………………….age: 53
6. Judy or Judith Guy…………………….age: 48
7. Silvy Guy…………………………….age: 45
8. Elizabeth Guy…………………………….age: 20
9. George Guy…………………………….age: 19
10. Amanda Anderson…………………….age: 25
11. Nathaniel Anderson…………………….age: 23
12. Mary Anderson…………………………….age: 21
13. Eliza Anderson…………………………….age: 21
14. Nancy Anderson…………………….age: 19

Guy

15. Cornelia Anderson..............................age: 18
16. William Washington Guy...................age: 30
17. Albert A Guy....................................age: 28
18. Amanda Guy....................................age: 26
19. Joseph M Guy..................................age: 24
20. Caroline T Guy................................age: 22
21. Martha Guy.....................................age: 25
22. Alexander Guy.................................age: 21
23. Sarah Guy.......................................age: 18
24. Garadine Guy..................................age: 12
25. George Guy....................................age: 11
26. Henrietta Guy..................................age: 9
27. Tennessee Guy................................age: 7
28. Ann Guy...age: 14
29. Rosa Guy..age: 12
30. McClelland Guy..............................age: 8
31. U S Guy or Wilford Grant Guy...........age: 7
32. Louisa Guy.....................................age: 8
33. John Guy..age: 6
34. Johnson Guy...................................age: 11
35. William Guy...................................age: 6
36. Katy Guy..age: 2
37. Peter Guy.......................................age: 40
38. Tabitha Steward..............................age: 50
39. Viney Guy......................................age: 48
40. Ann Gipson....................................age: 46
41. Katherine Guy.................................age: 45
42. Rachel Guy.....................................age: 43
43. June Bingham, married a white man........age: 41
44. George Guy....................................age: 28
45. Thomas Guy...................................age: 14
46. John Guy..age: 12
47. Henrietta Guy..................................age: 8
48. Mary Guy.......................................age: 23
49. Newton Guy...................................age: 16
50. Caroline Guy..................................age: 14
51. William Guy...................................age: 12
52. Ann Guy...age: 10
53. Daniel Guy.....................................age: 35

A Wandering Tribe

54. Mary Guy……………..………………..….age: 45
55. Charles Guy………………..……………….age: 18
56. George Guy…………………………...age: 16
57. Adaline Guy……………………………..age: 14
58. Brag Guy……………………………….age: 12
59. Judy Guy, daughter of Simon Jeffers………….age: 80
60. Edmond Guy……………………..………….age: 80
61. Willis Guy…………………………………...age: 61
62. Mahala Guy…………………………………age: 56
63. George W Guy………………………………age: 36
64. Mary S Guy…………………………………age: 33
65. Andrew T Guy………………………………age: 31
66. Martha Bingham, married a white man…………age: 27
67. Amanda M McDowell, married a white man…...age: 27
68. Joshua R Guy………………………………….age: 25
69. Amanda T Guy, white wife of Joshua R Guy…..age: 24
70. Erastus M Guy……………………….....………age: 3
71. Mary C Guy, white wife of A T Guy…age: 28
72. Henry H Guy……………………………age: 4
73. Emma F Guy………………………...……age: 2
74. Ruth M Guy…………………………age: 21
75. Sarah A Guy………………………….age: 19
76. Isaac H Guy……………………...………age: 17
77. Millard F Guy………………………….....age: 16
78. Lily R Guy……………………………………….age: 12
79. Samuel H McDowell, son of Amanda M, No. 67….age: 5
80. Eli H H J McDowell, son of Amanda M, No. 67…..age: 1
81. Elizabeth Guy, wife of G W Guy (white)…………age:30
82. Laurado Guy………………………………………...age: 4
83. Caly lee Guy…………………………………………age: 2
84. Charles Bingham, son of Martha, No. 66…………..age: 3

Those italicized desired permission of the president to settle in the Indian Territory, all of whom Mr. McDowell states were good and loyal people . . . their grandfathers on both sides assisted the government in the war for independence, and that their names were on muster rolls in the war department. William Guy, of Granville County, Georgia and Simon Jeffers of Bellville, Virginia, Cataw-

Guy

ba Indians, served 5 years in the Army, and were honorably discharged, and these 84 persons were their descendants. As these Indians were Catawbas and not Cherokees, Mr. McDowell was informed Oct. 22, 1872 that they could not receive any of the benefits arising from the Cherokee Removal fund of 1848. A schedule of 70 persons very similar to the foregoing list, each containing many of the same names, was forwarded to this office by Mr. McDowell, Oct. 19, 1869 (Misc. M. 1805), but for the same reason no relief could be granted them at that time more than in 1872."

A Wandering Tribe

**A Johnson Guy & Georgia A Gibson
Macon County, NC**

Guy

Sarah Adaline Guy
Daughter of Daniel & Mary Guy

A Wandering Tribe

1850 census of Macon County, NC:

Household # 100:

Guy, Buckner....mulatto...male......age: 57.......born: VA
Guy, Polly........mulatto...female....age: 26.......born: Orange, NC
Guy, Judith.......mulatto...female....age: 24........born: Macon, NC
Guy, Sylvia.......mulatto...female....age: 22........born: Macon, NC
Guy, Henry.......mulatto...male......age: 9.........born: Macon, NC

Household # 864:

Jeffreys, Walton...white......male...age: 52...born: VA
Jeffreys, Sylvia....white......male...age: 48....born: Caswell, NC
Jeffreys, Joshua J..white......male...age: 12...born: Macon, NC
Jeffreys, Lucy D...white......male....age: 9.....born: Macon,NC
Guy, John...........mulatto....male....age: 60....born: VA
Guy, Lucy S........mulatto....male....age: 40...born: Orange, NC
Guy, Creda E.......mulatto...male....age: 1.....born: Macon, NC

1860 census of Macon County, NC:

Household # 16:

Guy, Buckner F... mulatto...male....age: 63.....born: VA
Guy, Mary..........mulatto...female..age: 3......born: Orange, NC
Guy, Frida..........mulatto....female..age: 30.....born: Macon, NC
Guy, Silva...........mulatto...female...age: 25...born: Macon, NC
Guy, Henry J........mulatto...male.....age: 19...born: Macon, NC
Guy, Elizabeth......mulatto...female...age: 8.....born: Macon, NC
Guy, George.........mulatto...male.....age: 4.....born: Macon, NC
Guy, James..........mulatto...male.....age: 50...born: Macon, NC

Household # 291:

Guy, Daniel.........mulatto......male......age: 25....born: Macon, NC
Guy, Mary...........mulatto......female....age: 25....born: Ga
Guy, Charles W.....mulatto......male......age: 5......born: Macon, NC
Guy, George W...mulatto....male.....age: ......born: Macon, NC

Guy

Guy, Sarah A……mulatto…female…age: 1….born: .Macon, NC

Household # 609:

Guy, Clark……...mulatto…….male…….age: 46…born: Orange, NC
Guy, Catherine…mulatto…….female…...age: 40…born: Burke, NC
Guy, Joseph M…mulatto……..male…….age: 18…born: Macon, NC
Guy, Amanda E...mulatto…….female…...age: 14…born: Macon, NC
Guy, Carline T…..mulatto…….female…..age: 12…born: Macon, NC
Guy, Alexander C..mulatto……male…….age: 23…born: Macon, NC
Guy, Adaline…….mulatto…….male…….age: 23…born: Macon, NC

Household # 610:

Jeffers, Joshua……white……male………age: 22…born: Macon, NC
Jeffers, Martha E…white……female…….age: 24…born: Macon, NC
Jeffers, Marcus, M..white……male……….age: 5….born: Macon, NC
Jeffers, Harriet R….white……female…….age: 3….born: Macon, NC

Household # 611

Jeffery, Walton…..white…..male……...age: 70....born: Va
Jeffery, Silva……..white….female……age: 60…born: Caswell, NC
Jeffery, Isa D……..white….female……age: 1…..born: Macon, NC
Gipson, Stephen….mulatto..male……...age: 35….born: Haywood, NC

1870 census of Macon County, NC:

Household # 19:

Guy, Buckner……white………male……age: 77……born: VA
Guy, Mary……….white………female….age: 50……born: VA
Guy, Jude………..white………female….age: 40…….born: VA
Guy, Sylva……….white………female….age: 35……born: VA
Guy, Elizabeth…...white………male……age: 20…….born: NC
Guy, George L…..white………male……age: 15……born: NC
Guy, James………white……male……age: 58………….born: VA

A Wandering Tribe

George Guy
Grandson of Buckner Guy

Guy

1880 census of Macon County, North Carolina:

Household # 45:

Gipson, John………white……male……age: 26……...born: NC
Gipson, Elizabeth…mulatto…female…..age: 30……...born: NC
Gipson, Hiram……..white…...male…….age: 3………born: NC
Gipson, William…..white……male…….age: 1………born: NC

Household # 46:

Guy, George……mulatto……male……age: 25…….born: NC
Guy, Juda………mulatto……female….age: 50…….born: NC
Guy, James……..mulatto……male……age: 60…….born: NC
Guy, Polly……...mulatto……female….age: 55…….born: NC
Guy, Silby……...mulatto……female….age: 45…….born: NC
Guy, Nancy…….mulatto……female….age: 8……...born: NC

Household # 62:

Gibson, Hiram……white……..male……....age: 76……born: NC
Gibson, Margaret…white……..female……..age: 76…..born: NC
Gibson, Lee A…….white……..female……..age: 76…..born: NC
Gibson, Phereby E...white……..female……..age: 76…..born: NC
Gibson, Georgia Ann.. white….female……..age: 76…..born: NC
Pitts, Mary…………..white…….female……..age: 76…..born: NC
Pitts, John R………..white……..male……….age: 76…..born: NC
Jones, Walton……..white……..male…………age: 76….born: VA
Jones, Susan……….white……..female……..age: 76….born: SC
Gibson, Luvine…….white…….female……..age: 76…..born: NC

Household # 66:

Guy, Clark……..white……..male……….age: 60…..born: NC
Gibson, Harvey..white……..male……….age: 28…..born: NC
Gibson, Amanda.white…….female……..age: 39…..born: NC

Gibson, Johnson...white........male........age: 18......born: NC
Gibson, William...white........male........age: 14......born: NC
Gibson, Martha E...white.......female.......age: 9.......born: NC
Gibson, Hannah E..white.......female......age: 4.......born: NC
Gibson, Harvey.....white........male........age: 1.......born: NC

1900 census of Alculsa, Murray County, Georgia:

Household # 236:

Guy, George......white......male......age: 55......born: NC
Guy, Josephine...white......female....age: 36......born: NC
Guy, William.....white......male.......age: 16......born: NC
Guy, Julia M......white......female....age: 10......born: NC
Guy, Hester.......white......female....age: 2.........born: Tenn

**Tom Guy family
Orange County, NC**

HARRIS

Johnny Harris (born circa 1719 Cheraw Nation) a.k.a."Chuppepaw", a full-blooded Cheraw Indian, was the "King" of the Cheraw living within the Catawba Nation in the 1750's.

28 Oct 1738:
South Carolina Commissions of Indians:
"John Harris King of the Charraws"
"Captain Harris of Sugar Town"

1756:
Treaty between Virginia and the Catawba Indians:
Signer: Chippapaw

Harris the Tutelo (born approx. 1700 NC/VA border)
In 1882, John Buck, the last chief of the Tutelo among the Iroquois, reported that the Tutelo were led northward (to Canada) by a loyalist chief named Harris.

Allan Harris (born 1813, Catawba Reservation, SC) was a full-blooded Catawba Indian, the son of Sam Evans and Nancy Harris. Allan married Rhoda George, a white woman found as a child and raised by the Catawba. Allan Harris became Chief of the tribe and died in the Choctaw Nation, Indian Territory, in 1860 after he had journeyed there to survey a new reservation for the Catawba Nation.

Nancy Harris (born Jan 1851, Catawba Reservation, SC) was a ½ blood Catawba Indian, daughter of Chief Allan Harris and Rhoda George, a white woman adopted by the Catawba as a child.

1880 census for York County, SC (included those residing on the Catawba Reservation):

Household # 290:

Harris, Nancy……..Indian…..female….age: 30…..born: SC
Harris, Hillery…….Indian…..male…….age: 10…..born: SC
Harris, Agnes……...Indian…..female….age: 10…..born: SC

A Wandering Tribe

Harris, Lillie.........Indian......female....age: 7.......born: SC

Nancy Harris Starkey
1851-1919

1892:

Letter from A. E. Smith to Nancy Harris of Gainesville, Cooke County, Texas:

> "I am told by our member to the Legislature this year, that I am not allowed to pay any of the money appropriated by the state for support of Catawba Indians to those who are outside

the state...I would advise Agnes, if she thinks of going to you, to wait..."

1892 letter from Nancy Harris of Gainesville, Cooke County, Texas to South Carolina Governor R. Tillman:

"I have been informed by our agent A. E. Smith of Rock Hill, South Carolina, that the last session of legislature has passed an act of law to cut out me and my children of our just rights. And if it be so, God help them and preserve better heart in them, for trampling on our old forefather.
Our Agent, Mr. Smith, sent me and my children and grandchildren last year the small sum of $500 to Gainesville, Texas where I now live. Now Governor, if you please, look into this matter for me I would thank you very kindly if you will do so, to say whether we outside Catawbas ought to be deprived of our money and our rights there in the state of South Carolina. If we are, it is the first time since George Washington has laid down the flat farm to us. So I will close, wishing to hear direct from you. Yours respectfully, Nancy Harris, Catawba Indian, Gainesville, Cooke, Texas.'"

1900 census for Gainesville, Cooke County, Texas:

Household # 344:

Harris, Hillery...........white....male.......age: 29......born: SC
Harris, Mildred May...white....female.....age: 18......born: Tenn
Harris, Nancy............white...female.....age: 49......born: SC
Harris, Ella...............white...female.....age: 15......born: SC

On 3 Mar 1904, Nancy Harris married a white man, John Starkey in Cooke County, Texas. Nancy Harris Starkey died 16 Dec 1919 and is buried in Bradley, Grady County, Oklahoma.

1910 census for McClain, Turnbull County, Oklahoma:

Household # 179:

Harris, Hillery……white…..male………age: 40……….born: SC
Harris, Mary……...white…..female……age: 28………..born: Tenn
Starkey, Nancy…...white…..female…..age: 56…………born: SC

**Josiah A Harris
Sanford, Colorado.**

HART

Annie "Aruna" Hart Sizemore (born circa 1750, Catawba Reservation, SC) was at least half-blooded Catawba Indian, a daughter of James Hart. She married George Sizemore in Wilkes County, North Carolina circa 1770.

<u>**George Sizemore**</u>   <u>**Annie "Aruna" Hart**</u>

Children:

- Catherine "Dolly" Sizemore (born 1770) married James Hart
- John "Rock House" Sizemore (born 1771)
- Winnifred Minerva Sizemore (born 1772) married William T Begley
- Lydia Sizemore (born 1775) married James Blevins
- Sarah "Sallie" Sizemore (born 1776) married Elias Osborne
- George "Golden Hawk" Sizemore (b 1783)
- Edward B "Ned" Sizemore (born 1788) married Annie Baldwin
- Rhoda Sizemore (born 1789) married Aaron Brock
- Henry "Hunting Shirt" Sizemore (born 1790)
- Owen Sizemore (born 1793) married Rebecca Anderson
- Reverend George J Sizemore (born 1797) married Jennie Baldwin

[SEE SIZEMORE FAMILY FOR MORE INFORMATION]

John Hart (born 1819, Catawba Reservation, SC). John was among the group of Catawba who left South Carolina to live with the Cherokee after the Treaty of 1840. John was back in South Carolina by 1850, but had died enroute to Indian Territory in 1852.

Betsy Hart (born 1822, Catawba Reservation, SC). Betsy was living in South Carolina in 1849 but left with the party of Catawba enroute

A Wandering Tribe

to Indian Territory in 1852. Betsy Hart was adopted as a citizen of the Choctaw Nation on November 9th, 1853.

HEAD

Robert Henry Head (born 1841, Catawba Reservation, SC) was at least 1/4 Catawba and ¼ Pamunkey Indian, the son of an unknown white man and Lucy Mursh (born 1809 daughter of John Mursh and Betsy Scott). Robert enlisted in the Confederate Army, Company G, 5th South Carolina Infantry in 1862, and was deceased by 1863.

1860 census for York County, SC:

Household # 518:

Watts, Evans……..white……..male……..age: 49……..born: SC
Watts, Lucy………..white…….female……age: 40……..born: SC
Head, Robert H…...white…….male……..age: 18……..born: SC
Head, Emily Eliz….white……female……age: 16……...born: SC
Head, Peggy Jane…white……female……age:14……...born: SC
Head, John R……...white…..male……..age: 12……...born: SC
Watts, Nancy C……white……female……..age: 5……...born: SC
Watts, James H…….white…...male……..age: 2……...born: SC
Watts, W D………...white…...male……..age: 1……...born: SC
Timms, John L……..white…...male……..age: 14……...born: SC

A Wandering Tribe

Robert Henry Head

Pinkney Henry Head (born Oct 1862, Catawba Reservation, SC) was a 5/8-blooded Catawba – 1/8-blooded Paumnkey Indian, the son of Robert Henry Head and Sarah Louisa Evans. Pinkney H Head married Martha Jane Patterson. Martha Jane Patterson (born 21 Nov 1868

Head

Catawba Reservation, SC) was a half-blood Catawba Indian, daughter of James G Patterson and Elizabeth Missouri White.

1880 census for York County, SC (included those residing on the Catawba Reservation):
Household # 311:
Head, Sarah.............Indian.....female....age: 37.....born: SC
Head, Pinckney........Indian.....male.......age: 18.....born: SC

January 9, 1896:
Letter from Senator H. M. Teller to the Commissioner of Indian Affairs:
"...enclosed a letter from P. H. Head, a Catawba Indian of Sanford, Colorado, submitting a petition purporting to have been signed by himself and twenty-five others, embracing six Catawba families once resident in South Carolina but who were no longer recognized by that state, asking to be united with the Ute Indian Tribe living on the Uintah reservation in Utah."

1900 census for Conejos, Sanford County, Colorado:

Household # 55:

Head, Pinky H.......white.....male..........age: 33.....born: SC
Head, Martha J.....white.....female........age: 31.....born: SC
Head, Sarah.........white.....female........age: 13.....born: SC
Head, Lucy M......white.....female........age: 11......born: Colorado
Head, Hattie.........white.....female........age: 6.......born: Colorado
Head, Heber.........white.....male..........age: 5......born: Colorado
Head, Willard.......white.....male...........age: 3......born: Colorado
Head, Nellie.........white....female........age: 1.......born: Colorado

1910 census for San Juan, Farmington County, New Mexico:

Household # 332: [all originally marked as "mixed" then crossed through and written in as "Indian"]

Head, Pickney......Indian.....male......age: 47....born: SC
Head, Martha.......Indian.....female....age: 42....born: SC

Head, Lucy………Indian…..female….age: 18….born: Colorado
Head, Hefner…….Indian…..male……age: 14….born: Colorado
Head, Willard…....Indian…..male……age: 12….born: Colorado
Head, Nellie……..Indian….female…..age: 10….born: Colorado
Head, George…....Indian…..male…….age: 8…..born: Colorado
Head, Helen……..Indian…..female…..age: 6…..born: New Mexico
Head, Harry….Indian…..male……age: 4……..born: New Mexico
Head, Mary….Indian…..female…..age: 1……..born: New Mexico

1920 census for San Juan, Farmington County, New Mexico:

Household # 23:

Head, Pinkney…white…..male….....age: 56……..born: SC
Head, Martha… white…..female….age: 54……..born: SC
Head, Willard…white…..male……age: 22……..born: Colorado
Head, Nellie…...white….female….age: 20……...born: Colorado
Head, George….white…..male……age: 19……..born: Colorado
Head, Helen……white….female…age: 16……...born: New Mexico
Head, Harry……white….male……age: 13……..born: New Mexico
Head, Mary…….white…..female…age: 10……..born: New Mexico
Head, Dorothy....white…..female…age: 8……….born: New Mexico
Beals, Arthur…..white…..male…...age: 19……..born: Colorado

1930 census for San Juan, Farmington County, New Mexico:

Household # 23:

Head, Pinkney…Indian…..male…….age: 67…….born: SC
Head, Martha..….Indian…..female….age: 61…….born: SC
Head, Willard…Indian…..male……age: 34……..born: Colorado
Head, George…..Indian…..male…….age: 28…….born: Colorado
Head, Harry…….Indian…..male…….age: 23……born: New Mexico
Head, Mary…….Indian…..female….age: 20……born: New Mexico
Head, Dorothy….Indian…..female…..age: 18…….born: New Mexico

Head

**James Patterson (left) and Heber Head (right)
Sanford County, Colorado**

March 16, 1939:

Letter from Pinkney Head to the President of the United States, Washington D.C.:

> Sir: I am one of the committee of Catawba Indians living in the west. Our former was in the State of South Carolina. I enclose for your consideration a copy from the Congressional

A Wandering Tribe

hearing of a few years ago regards our people. There are about 100 of our people living in the west.

The State of South Carolina has not lived up to the treaties made with my tribe and we want them to do so. These treaties date from 1806 and 1815. The state leased the Indian lands for 99 years or three lives at 15 and 20 cents per acre, payable annually, amounting to 5000 dollars annually and have not paid this amount or anything approximating it.

We wish to now make a final settlement with the tribe and leave the jurisdiction of the state and be turned over to the Federal government. The back rentals should be paid up before the final settlement is agreed upon.

We are the only tribe in the U.S. that the Government has not been compelled to fight at one time or another. In this old treaty it was promised that land would be secured for us in Oklahoma and North Carolina and Arkansas. We went to all these places looking for land but found that no provision had been made and most of our tribe went back. I have a history of part of this scheme to get my people away so the state could keep these lands.

What we want is our rights given to us according to these treaties.

Will you kindly look into this matter for me and let me know what you can do.

Very sincerely, P. H. Head

Head

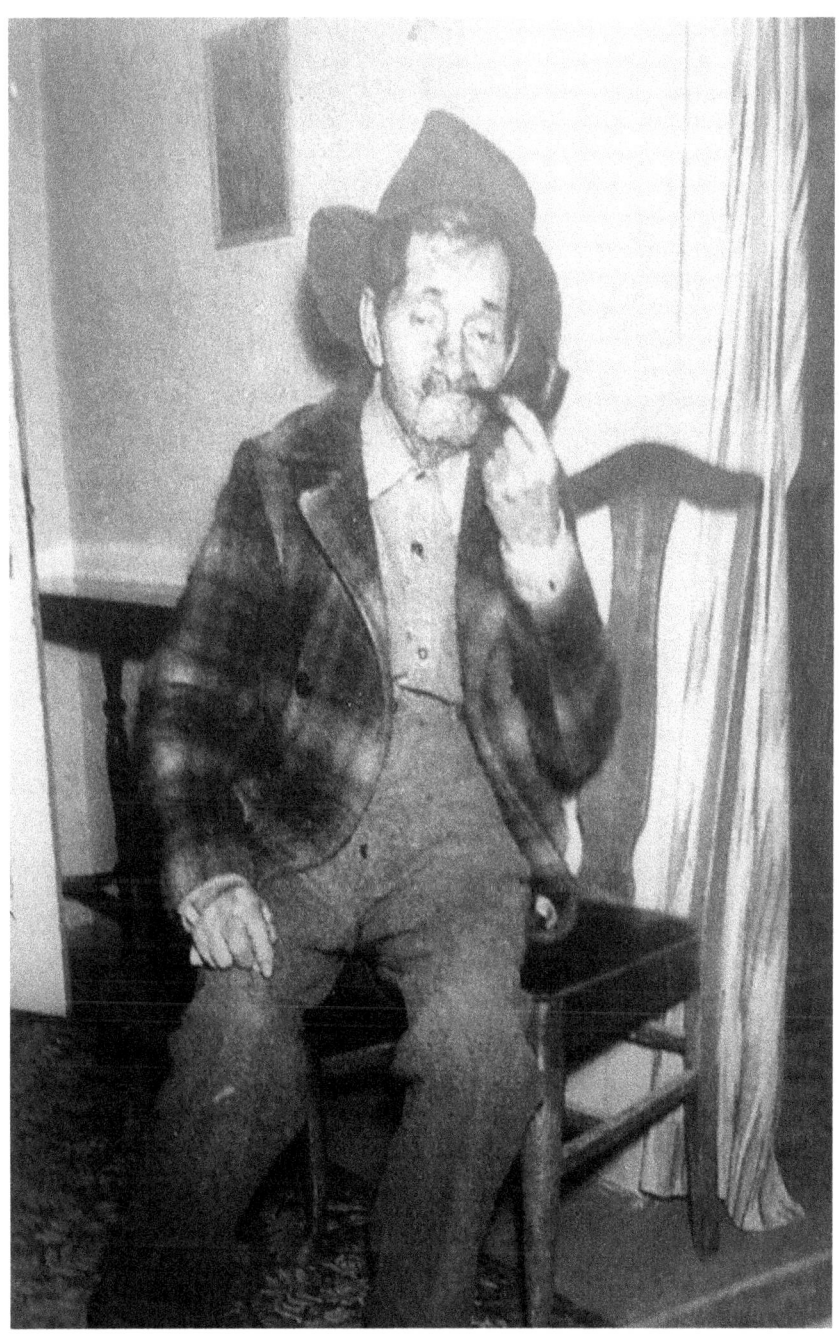

Pinkney Head
Farmington, New Mexico

JEFFRIES

1736 to 1742:

Brafferton Indian school at William & Mary:
Indian student: Will Jeffries

Simon Jeffries (born 1756 Greensville County, VA, died 1773 Mecklenburg County, VA) was at least ½ Catawba Indian.

28 Jan 1790:

Greensville Co. bond, Minister's Returns, p.19:
Andrew "Drury" Jeffries married Silvia Scott.

Parker Jeffries

A Wandering Tribe

1842:

Parker Jeffries V. Ohio, Ohio Supreme Court, Greene County, Ohio:

> Parker Jeffries was refused the right to vote. The jury found "that the plaintiff is of the Indian race, the illegitimate son of a white man and a woman of the Indian race, and that he has not more than one fourth of the Indian blood in his veins."

1881:

"History of Greene County, Ohio" by R. F. Dill:

> ….James Jeffreys, furniture manufacturer….was born in Greeneville, Virginia, January 30, 1821….son of Silas and Susan (Pruitt) Jeffries. Silas was a descendant of the Catawba tribe of Indians…Mason Jeffreys….born in Cedarville (Ohio) September 8, 1835, and is the son of Uriah and Caroline Jeffreys, who were born in North Carolina, and came to this county about 1830. Uriah was a descendant of the tribe of Catawba Indians.

James Jeffries

Jeffries

Oct 1869:

Letter from Dr. Joseph McDowell to Eli Parker, U.S. Commissioner of Indian Affairs:

> ...I take the Liberty of addressing to you a few lines on behalf of a remnant of the tribe of Catawba Indians...Some 60 or 70 years since they left their tribe and went to Greenville County, Virginia, and then removed to Orange County, North Carolina...they sold out in Orange and moved to Macon County, N.C. where they purchased land and remained every since.

Oct 1872:

U.S. Senate Document #144, entitled "The Catawba Tribe of Indians":

> ....Dr. Joseph McDowell, of Fairmont, GA, asking relief of the Government...Catawba Indians, and 81 in number...wishing the government to assist them in moving west to Indian Territory...William Guy, of Granville County, Ga (sic NC), and Simon Jeffries, of Bellville, Virginia, Catawba Indians, served five years in the Army and were honorably discharged, and these people are their descendants.

1850 census of Macon County, NC:

Household # 864:

Jeffreys, Walton.....white......male...age: 52......born: VA
Jeffreys, Sylvia......white......male...age: 48......born: Caswell, NC
Jeffreys, Joshua J....white........male...age: 12......born: Macon, NC
Jeffreys, Lucy D......white......male...age: 9.......born: Macon,NC
Guy, John.............mulatto...male...age: 60......born: VA
Guy, Icy S............mulatto....male...age: 40......born: Orange, NC
Guy, Creda E.........mulatto...male...age: 1.......born: Macon, NC

1860 census of Macon County, NC:

Household # 612:

A Wandering Tribe

Jeffrey, Walton….white……male…age: 70….born: VA
Jeffrey, Silva…….white……male…age: 60….born: Caswell, NC
Jeffrey, Isa D…….white……male…age: 18….born: Macon, NC
Gibson, Stephen…mulatto….male…age: 35….born: Haywood, NC

**Margaret "Peggy" Jones
(daughter of Walton Jones & Sylvia Jeffries)
& husband, Hiram Gibson
Macon County, NC**

JOHNSON

Tama Johnson (born circa 1830) was a full-blooded Catawba Indian.

21 May 1937:

Interview of George McIntosh, Oklahoma Indian Pioneer Interviews, Volume 58:

> …Information about mother: Tama Johnson McIntosh. She was a Catawba Indian, married to Tobe McIntosh at the Creek Agency after the slaves were made free.

Francis (Ferrell) Johnson (born circa 1800 Colleton District, SC) was a full-blooded Indian of unknown tribal origin.

15 Oct 1849:

Affidavit of Miss Ann Duval of Colleton District, SC:

> …She well knew one George Ferrell to have resided in said district [Colleton] during the time she lived there…he was always taken for a Free Indian. He had a sister named Francis who intermarried with one Parker, who died. She afterwards married one James Johnson who was a white man. Francis was a free Indian.

12 Nov 1849:

Affidavit of John Edwards of Colleton District, SC:

> ….Francis Ferrell intermarried with one Parker likewise a free Indian. The said Francis Parker otherwise Francis Johnson and the said James Johnson have long since died.

December 1860:

A Wandering Tribe

Affidavit of Mrs. Margaret E. Gordon of Charleston District, SC:

> …she was acquainted with Eve Johnson the mother of Ellen Burckmeyer, that she has known her for forty years and upwards past, that she was of Indian descent.

KEGG

William Cask/Cagg (born circa 1710 SC) signed the 1759 petition of Catawba Indians.

1780-81:

"Capt Thomas Drennans company of Catawba Indians"

Signor: John Cagg [Kegg]
Signor: Billey Cagg [Kegg]

November 24, 1792:

Petition of "the Chief and Head Men of Cataba Nation":
General New River
Signor: Captain John Cagg [Kegg]

James "Jamey" Kegg (born 1783 Catawba Reservation, SC) was a full-blooded Catawba Indian. He married Jenny Scott (daughter of General New River and Sally Toole) circa 1816, also a full-blooded Catawba Indian.

Jamey Kegg had two known sons, Phillip Kegg and James Kegg, and two daughters, Betsy Kegg and Susy Kegg. All four children joined with the portion of the tribe that removed to the Cherokee in western NC. Betsy and Susy both married Cherokees and remained among the Cherokee, however Phillip continued west to Indian Territory.

1840: Commissioners for the Treaty of Nation Ford report:

....Jamey Kegg now claims the Generalship [sic Chief position] he being their senior about 55 years of age and being a full blooded Indian and the only descendant of the Newriver family.

James "Jamey" Kegg died in the St. Luke's Indian Settlement in the fall of 1862.

Phillip Kegg (born 1822 Catawba Reservation, SC) a full-blooded Catawba Indian, son of James "Jamey" Kegg and Jenny Scott.

1885 Choctaw Nation census, San Bois County, Indian Territory:

#465 Kegg, Phillip......Indian....male....age: 63........farmer

James "Jim" Kegg Jr (born circa 1843 Cherokee Reservation, NC) a full-blooded Catawba Indian, son of James "Jamey" Kegg and Jenny Scott. James served in the Confederacy during the Civil War in Thomas' Legion, the North Carolina Cherokee Battalion, 69th NC Regiment.

March 28, 1896:

Letter of Department of the Interior, Office of Indian Affairs, Washington, DC:

> "On the 21st of November, 1887, James Kegg, of Whittier, North Carolina, in addressing the Secretary of the Interior (# 31383), made the following statement, viz: 'Many years ago, his people, the Catawba Indians, leased the land they owned in

Kegg

South Carolina and became a wondering tribe without homes for their wives and children. They made applications he states, to the Cherokees of North Carolina for homes upon their land . . . that about 500 or so were adopted . . . that some 300 or so were removed west under the Cherokee treaty of New Echota. Those Catawba remaining in South Carolina, Mr. Kegg states, had no interest whatever, in the lands which were leased out by those who became Cherokee by adoption."

1900 Special Indian census of OconeeLuftee Township, Swain County, North Carolina:

Household # 23:

Kegg, James a.k.a. Jae-mee Sa-Taw-nee…Indian…male…age: 57…born: NC Tribe of this Indian: Cherokee Tribe of Father: Cherokee Tribe of mother: Catawba

Kegg, Katee a.k.a. Ku-Ta-Kee………Indian……female……age: 47…….born: NC Tribe of this Indian: Cherokee Tribe of Father: Cherokee Tribe of mother: Cherokee

After 1900 (undated) U.S. Indian Census Rolls, Eastern Band of Cherokee, North Carolina:

Household # 500:

Kegg, Jim…………….male………..husband…………….age: 61
Kegg, Katy…………..female……..wife……………….age: 54
Kegg, Matthew……male………..son……………….age: 39

A Wandering Tribe

James "Jim" Kegg Jr (marked by arrow) at the 1903 Confederate reunion in New Orleans.

KENNEDY

Johnston (John) Kennedy (born Catawba Reservation, SC) was at least ½ blood Catawba Indian. After 1813 he married his second wife, Betsy Ayers, whose father was Jacob Ayers and mother was the daughter of King Hagler (former wife of William Scott and Matthew Toole).

1792:

Petition of Catawba Indians to the Governor of South Carolina: Signor: John Kennedy

March 28 1793:

Records of Governor Moultrie, South Carolina:

> "Whereas I have received information from the Agents appointed to take care of the Rights of the Catawba Indians that a Prosecution has been commenced against several of the said Indians in the Court of the County of Lancaster, to Wit, Patrick Redhead, Jenny Patterson and John Kennedy for trading with Negroes and that it is apprehended that the said Court intends to inflict Corporal Punishment on them. Now know ye that in consideration of the said Indians being Free People and under the protection of this State I do by these Presents pardon and release said Indians from any Judgment or punishment whatever which has been or may be ordered to be inflicted on them by the said Court of which all concerned are to take due Notice and govern themselves accordingly."

Richard Kennedy (born 1800 Catawba Reservation, SC) was at least ½ blood Catawba Indian. He first married Nancy Brown, then married Elizabeth Chavers.

A Wandering Tribe

In the early 1800's Catawba Indians began leasing plots of their reservation land to white land speculators. Records of these leases were recorded in a "Plat Book", only one of which has survived.

Catawba Reservation Leases Plat Book:

Tenant:	Receiver of Lease Payments:
William Partlow	Johnston Kennedy
William Jackson	Johnston Kennedy
James Harris & Johnston Kennedy	divided between William RedHead
William Pettus	divided between Betsy Kennedy & Billy Canty
Estate of James Harris	Richard Kennedy

[Catawba Plat Book pages 191, 213, 259].

Richard Kennedy appears in Catawba Plat Book leases from 1813 to 1826, after which he left the reservation and disappears from any Catawba records.

The evidence lent by the Catawba Plat Books, dates of leases, and Richard taking over lease payments for the older Johnston, weighs that Richard Kennedy was the son of Johnston (John) Kennedy and Betsy Kennedy.

Richard Kennedy married Nancy Brown, daughter of John Genet Brown (Catawba Indian) [Catawba Plat Book page 222]. Nancy Brown died in **July 1824**. Shortly after, Richard Kennedy left the reservation and their only child was taken in by Nancy George. Nancy Brown Kennedy's lease payments were signed over to Nancy George for support of the minor child. There was an entry of "Richard Kennedy Indian Boy" in the Plat Book on **July 10, 1823**, so the child was most likely male and named for his father [Catawba Plat Book Page 177]. Whether this child died young, or assumed a different surname and lived on among the Catawba, is not recorded.

In 1840 Richard Kennedy is recorded on the 1840 census of Chester District, South Carolina, less than five miles from the reservation, where he had found work as a laborer. The census recorded his name but placed no mark in either the "Free Whites" column, nor in the "Free Colored" column.

December 18, 1840:

South Carolina Legislature confirms the Treaty of Nation Ford. Ending the leasing rent payments.

It is apparent that Richard Kennedy took what rent payments he had saved and, along with his new wife (Elizabeth Chavers – Kennedy estate papers reflect that Richard and Elizabeth "Intermarried in North Carolina") crossed the Savannah River into Georgia (most likely to live next to Elizabeth's sister, Sarah Chavers Hosford, as the birth locations of Sarah's children indicate she had been living in Georgia from 1832 to 1848). Birth locations of his children indicate that the Kennedy family resided in Georgia from 1841 to 1848. Sometime in 1848-49, Richard Kennedy, his wife Elizabeth Chavers Kennedy, as well as his sister-in-law Sarah Chavers Hosford, crossed the border into Alabama and settled in Henry County.

In all existent documentation, Richard signed his name as "Richard Kenaday" [Alabama Estate Files, 1830-1976].

November 1, 1858:

"Richard Kenady" recorded his plot of 80 and 5/100 acres at:

"the Northeast quarter of the South East quarter of Section Twenty six and the North East quarter of the North East quarter of Section Thirty five in Township five North of Range Twenty six East, in the District of Alabama of lands subject to sale at Elba, Alabama."

June 25, 1862:

Richard Kennedy died in Henry County, Alabama.

His estate papers specifically identified his heirs as: "Dempsey Kennedy, Calvin Kennedy, Elizabeth Kennedy Whitehead, Cristenberry Kennedy, Nancy Ann Kennedy Smith, Piercy Kennedy (a minor at Richard's death), Barny Kennedy, Alabama Kennedy, Henry Kennedy."

Richard Kennedy   Elizabeth Chavers

Children:

- Dempsey Kennedy (born 1830) married Nancy Whitehead
- Nancy Ann Kennedy (born 1833) married William Smith
- Elizabeth Kennedy Whitehead (born 1834) married Henry Whitehead
- Barney Kennedy (born 1835) married (1st) Rusney (?) then (2nd) Sarah Chance
- Alabama Kennedy (born 1837)
- Henry Kennedy (born 1839) married Susan (?)
- Christenberry Kennedy (born 1841) married Mahala Mills
- Calvin Kennedy (born 1843) married Hester Anderson
- Piercy Kennedy (born 1848)

1850 census of Henry County, Alabama:

Household # 106:

Kenedy, Richd…………white….male…..age: 50……b: NC
Kenedy, Elizabeth……...white…female...age: 47……b: NC

Kennedy

Kenedy, Demcy…..…...white….male…..age: 20…...b: NC
Kenedy, Ann J………...white…..female…age: 17…...b: NC
Kenedy, Elizabeth……...white….female…age: 16…..b: SC
Kenedy, Barny…………white…..male…...age: 15…...b: SC
Kenedy, Alabama……...white…..female…age: 13…...b: SC
Kenedy, Henry………...white…..male…..age: 11…....b: SC
Kenedy, Christenberry...white…...male….age: 9……..b: GA
Kenedy, Calvin………..white……male….age: 7……..b: GA
Kenedy, Pearcy………..white……male…age: 2……...b: GA

Household # 107:
Chavis, Sarah……...white……..female……age: 43……b: NC
Chavis, Betsy……..white……..female……age: 18…….b: GA
Chavis, Martha……white……..female……age:12…….b: GA
Chavis, Jasper……..white……..male………age: 9…….b: GA
Chavis, Newton……white……..male………age: 7…….b: GA
Chavis, Francis M…white……..male………age: 4…….b: GA

1860 Census, Henry County, Alabama:

Household # 07:

Cannada, [sic Kennedy] Dempsey…Black….male….age: 26...b: GA
Cannada, Nancy………..Mulatto..…female…age: 26...b: GA
Cannada, William………Mulatto..…male…..age: 5….b: ALA
Cannada, Richard……….Mulatto..…male…..age: 2….b: ALA
Cannada, Elizabeth……..Mulatto….female….age: 1....b: ALA

Household # 78:

Ivins [sic Evans], John……..Black……male…….age: 32…....b: SC
Ivins [sic Evans], Nancy……Black……female….age: 32…....b: GA
Ivins [sic Evans], Elizabeth..Black…….female…..age: 4……..b: GA
Ivins [sic Evans], Elmedy….Black…….female…age: 1……..b: ALA
Cannada, [sic Kennedy]…...Mulatto..…female…..age: 24…...b: ALA
Cannada, James………..Mulatto……male……..age: 3……...b: ALA
Cannada, Thomas…….Mulatto……male……..age: 2………..b: ALA

1860 census of Milton, Santa Rosa, FL:

A Wandering Tribe

Household # 174:

Kennedy, B B [Barney]…..mulatto..male……age: 25……….b: NC
Kennedy, Rusney…………mulatto...female…age: 21…..……b: Ga
Kennedy, Mariella………..mulatto...female…age: 25……….b: Ala
Kennedy, Ruebin J………..mulatto...male…...age: 10……….b: Ala
Kennedy, Lalona………….mulatto...female….age: 8………..b: Ala
Kennedy, R. P…………….mulatto...male……age: 1…..……b: Ala

1870 census of Monroe County, Alabama:

Household # 986:

Kennedy, Elisha……….Indian….male…..age: 55…...b: NC
Kennedy, Barney..……..Indian….male…..age: 30…...b: Ala
Kennedy, Ann………….Indian….female….age: 15…..b: Ala
Kennedy, Dolphin…..….Indian….male…...age: 14…..b: Ala
Kennedy, Mary…..…….Indian….female….age: 2…….b: Ala

1870 Census, Henry County, Alabama:

Household 185:

Chavis, Sarah…....Mulatto…..female….age: 65………..b: SC
Chavis, Jasper…..Mulatto..….male….age: 30…..…...…b: GA
Chavis, Franklin..Mulatto……male…..age: 22………..b: GA

Household 186:

Chavis, Mary A……..Mulatto…female….age: 32…..b: GA
Chavis, John………..Mulatto…male…....age: 16…..b: ALA
Chavis, Sarah……….Mulatto…female.....age: 12…..b: ALA

Household 187:

Kennedy, Nancy …..Mulatto……female…..age: 35…b: ALA
Kennedy, William....Mulatto…….male…....age: 15....b: ALA

Kennedy

Kennedy, Margaret...Mulatto......female.....age: 13...b: ALA
Kennedy, Richard....Mulatto.......male........age:12....b: ALA
Kennedy, John.........Mulatto.......male........age: 9.....b: ALA
Kennedy, Rody........Mulatto......female.......age:4.....b: ALA
Kennedy, Matthew...Mulatto.......male........age: 2.....b: ALA

3 sons of Richard Kennedy & Elizabeth Chavers Kennedy served in the Confederate Army, 39th Alabama Infantry Regiment Company D: Barney Kennedy, Calvin Kennedy, & Henry Kennedy. 2 sons of Sarah Chavers served in the Confederate Army, 39th Alabama Infantry Regiment Company D: Jasper Chavers, & Newton Chavers.

After the conclusion of the Civil War, several of the Kennedy/Chavers family moved slightly west:

1870 Census, Monroe County, Alabama:

Household 986:

Kennedy, Elisha [sic Dempsy...Indian....male.....age: 55...b:NC
Kennedy, Barny....................Indian....male.....age: 30..b: ALA
Kennedy, Dolphies...............Indian.....female...age: 1...b: ALA
Kennedy, Mary....................Indian....female...age: 14..b: ALA

1880 Census, Escambia County, Alabama:

Household 144:

Kennedy, Henry....................Indian....male....age:... 44....b: GA
Kennedy, Susan...................Indian....female...age: ..28....b: FL
Kennedy, Mary....................Indian.....female....age: 11....b: ALA
Kennedy, Rocksy A...............Indian.....female...age: 9.....b: ALA

A Wandering Tribe

Kennedy, James………………….Indian..…..male…...age: 3…..b: ALA
Kennedy, Virginia……………....Indian…….female...age: 3….b: ALA
Kennedy, Elizabeth [Chavers]....Indian…....female....age: 8….b: SC

March 30, 1885:
Sarah Chavers recorded a homestead deed to 160 acres in Henry County, Alabama at:

> "1 East ½ North West Saint Stephen's South. North 26 East 36; 2 West ½ North East Saint Stephen's South, North 26 East 36."

June 25, 1886:

Sarah Chavers transferred the entire deed over to her son, Jasper Chavers.

Nov 3, 1971:

Letter from Calvin Beale (ethnologist) recording his conversation with Chief Calvin McGhee (of the Poarch Creeks):
[Chief McGhee had visited the Kennedy/Chavers Indian Community at Wild Fork and tried to convince them that they were descendants of Creek Indians and should sign up for the Creek Land Claims case. McGhee was rebuffed when the people of the community denied knowledge of any Creek Indian ancestry, and instead claimed to be descendants of the Catawba Nation.]

> *…McGhee said that the Chavers people did not really know who they were. But one elderly woman of the group told him they came from the Carolinas and were Catawbas.*

Kennedy

Richard P Kennedy

A Wandering Tribe

**Chavers Indian School
Wildfork, Monroe County, Alabama**

LERBLANCE

Elijah Hermigine Lerblance (born March 1836) was a ¼ blood Catawba Indian. He was adopted into the Creek Nation in Indian Territory and became a Muskogee District Judge and served in the House ofKings of the Creek Nation.

31 June 1937:

Interview of Willie Lerblance, Oklahoma Indian Pioneer Interviews, Volume 53:

> *My grandfather was Elija Hermigine Lerblance (La Blanche). He was born in March 1836, son of a Louisiana Frenchman, and Vicey Gentry, who was the daughter of Elijah Gentry (Colonel E.W. Gentry), a white who married a full-blood Catawba Indian. He came from Alabama to the Creek Nation with his parents at the age of 12 years (came into Indian Territory in approx. 1848).*

1891:

Leaders and Leading Men of the Indian Territory, by H F O'Beirne:

> The subject of this sketch was born in March 1836, and is the son of Hermogene Lerblance, a Louisiana Frenchman, and Vicey Gentry, daughter of Elijah Gentry, a white man who married a full-blood Catawba Indian. The subject of this sketch moved from Alabama to the Creek Nation, with his parents, at the age of twelve, after which he attended the Asberry Mission Manual Labor School for a term of fifteen months. At the age of seventeen years he commenced learning the blacksmith trade, and while thus employed he married Miss Bosen, daughter of Amos Bosen, King of the Hitchetee

A Wandering Tribe

Town. By this marriage he had five children, W. P., born June 17, 1856; F. W., born November 10, 1858; Sarah, born December 10, 1860; W. L., born March 23, 1864; and Jeannette, born July 4, 1866. His wife died a devout Christian and member of the M. E. Church, in 1872. In 1857 Mr. Lerblance moved to Cussetah, where he worked in the government blacksmith shop until the outbreak of the war in 1861, when he joined the Confederate service as a private, was made sergeant in three months, and in 1862 rose to the rank of lieutenant, which office he held until the termination of the war. Afterwards he returned with his family to the farm he had commenced to improve, near the old council grounds, in the Creek Nation, his property consisting of an old wagon, a pair of oxen, two cows and calves, one pig and thirty-five cents in cash. From this time until 1880 he spent his life partly on the farm and partly in the blacksmith shop. In 1881 he embarked in the cattle business with W. E. Gentry, the title of the firm being W. E. Gentry & Co., the result of the partnership at this date being 2,500 head of cattle, one store in Checotah, with a stock of general merchandise amounting to $12,000, one gin at the same place, the house occupied by the druggist, C. G. Moore, at Checotah, as well as about a half interest in the Indian Journal, published at Eufaula. In February 1878, Mr. Lerblance married Miss Nellie Fife, daughter of Job Fife, a farmer and son of Jimmie Fife, of noted fame in Pigott's History. The surviving issue of this marriage is Francis H., born December 2, 1879; Addie, born September 26, 1882; Howard P., born November 17, 1885, and Lizzie C., born April 29, 1888. Mr. Lerblance owns one of the finest residences in the vicinity of Hitchetee, 200 acres of farm, one square mile of pasture, 400 head of cattle, 50 mules and horses, a large stock of hogs, and a comfortable home in Checotah. Mr. Lerblance served four years as Clerk of Muskogee District and eight years as Supreme Court Clerk. At three different periods he

Lerblance

served as District Judge of Muskogee District. He was once elected National Treasurer, but declined to serve. In 1891 he filled the unexpired term of Samuel Bradley, in the House of Kings, who died in May of that year. Mr. Lerblance was opposed to the sale of Oklahoma, fearing it would cause the opening of the entire Indian Territory. He thought it would be wiser to use it for grazing purposes, and thereby secure funds sufficient to satisfy the United States Government for her claim on said lands, originating under treaty of 1866. Judge Lerblance is a gentleman of good address, pleasant manners, and intellectually far above the average. As a businessman he has few superiors, as will become plain to those who read his record. He also bears an excellent reputation as a judge, and taken on the whole, there are few men who stand bigger in his nation than E. H. Lerblance.

Elijah H Lerblance

LOGAN

George Logan (born 1777 Charleston, SC) was at least ½ Catawba Indian.

28 July 1807:

Affidavit of John Gough of St. Phillips, Charleston, SC:

> ...*made oath that George Logan, a free man of colour, was born in Charleston in the year 1777 of a free Indian woman of the Catawba Nation.*

LUCAS

Charles Lucas, Jr (born 1771 north east side of the Pee Dee River, Dillon, South Carolina) According to family lore, Charles Lucas, Jr's mother was one "Dorcas, a Catawba Indian". Charles Daniel Lucas, Sr. is found on the 1790 census as residing in Robeson County, North Carolina, so there is a strong possibility that his "Catawba wife" may have had connections to one of the numerous Indian families now known as the "Lumbee".

Charles Lucas, Jr. left South Carolina and journeyed west to Alabama where he became a Federal Indian Agent to the Creeks. Having died in Fayette County, Alabama, his body was interred within an old Indian burial ground, his lone stone marker surrounded by more primitive Indian burials. Of final remarkable note are the several Lucas individuals who appear as "Indian" on the early census of Baldwin and Mobile Counties of Alabama, either living with, or in close confines to, the Creek half-bloods whose ancestors today are the Poarch Band of Creeks.

A Wandering Tribe

Eady Lucas Goins (born: before 1780 Catawba Reservation, SC, died before 1830 Sumter, SC) was at least ½ Catawba Indian. Eady Lucas married Jeremiah Goins in Berkeley District, SC.

Aug 1893:

Interview of Rebecca Jacobs by McDonald Furman, Sumter, SC:

> *...[Eady Lucas Goins] said she came from the Catawba tribe.*

MORRISON

William Morrison (born 1815 Catawba Reservation, SC) was a full-blooded Catawba Indian and was married to Mary Scott. William was Chief of the Catawba tribe beginning at least in 1844 and led the portion of the tribe that left South Carolina to live with the Cherokee in western North Carolina in 1848. William Morrison petitioned to be adopted into the Choctaw Nation, Indian Territory, on 9 Nov 1853. Two of William's sons, Thomas and John, left with him and eventually they ended up in Indian Territory and petitioned to be adopted into the Choctaw Nation.

Thomas Morrison (born 1836 Catawba Reservation, SC) a full-blooded Catawba Indian, son of Chief William Morrison and Mary Scott. Thomas appears on the 1849 census of Catawba Indians living in Haywood County, NC among the Cherokee. William Morrison petitioned to be adopted into the Choctaw Nation, Indian Territory, on 9 Nov 1853. In 1886 Thomas Morrison returned to South Carolina and became Chief of the Catawba Tribe.

James "Jim" Morrison (born 1810, Catawba Reservation, SC) was a full-blooded Catawba Indian, older brother of Chief William Morrison. In 1850 he was living in Beaufort District Indian Settlement and married to Sarah Bing.

1854:

Report to the Governor of South Carolina on the Catawba Indian by Agent B.S. Massey:

> *"Jim Morrison and child left for Charleston about 1851, last heard from 1853."*

1850 census for St. Luke's Parish, Beaufort County, SC:

A Wandering Tribe

Household # 284:

Morrison, James……..mulatto…..male……..age: 40…..born: SC
Morrison, Sarah……..mulatto…..female…….age: 40…..born: SC
Morrison, James…….mulatto…..male………..age: 17…..born: SC

1860 census for St. Luke's Parish, Beaufort County, SC:

Household # 357
:
Morrison, James……..mulatto…..male……..age: 54…..born: SC
Morrison, Sarah……..mulatto…..female…….age: 58…..born: SC
Household # 211:

Morrison, James A…..mulatto……..male…….age: 26…….born: SC
Morrison, Elvina………mulatto……..female….age: 23……born: SC
Morrison, Ann…………mulatto……..female…..age: 1……..born: SC

1870 census for Gillsonville, Beaufort County, SC:

Household # 284:

Morrison, James……..mulatto…..male……..age: 61…..born: SC
Morrison, Sarah……...mulatto…..female…...age: 65…..born: SC
Taylor, Nelly………...mulatto…..female…...age: 68…..born: SC

James Morrison left a written will in Beaufort County, signed and submitted by him on 27 March 1880. In his will he mentions he had two living children on that date, Sarah Leonara and John Hampton, and his real estate included "one house and lot in the village of Gillsonville consisting originally of about one fourth of an acre, to which I subsequently added five acres more, one lot in the village of Grahamville containing two acres - One tract of land called the "Bing Tract" containing about One Hundred acres and one tract called the "Morrison old Homestead" containing about Two Hundred acres."

PATTERSON

James Goodwin Patterson (born 8 Nov 1849, Catawba Reservation, SC) was a quarter-blood Catawba, the son of Laban Chapell and half-blood Catawba Martha Patterson. James Patterson married Elizabeth Missouri White (born 3 Sept 1849, Catawba Reservation, SC) a full-blooded Catawba Indian, daughter of George White and Margaret Marsh.

24 April 1877:

> "Catawba Indians requesting William White of Rock Hill to be their agent."
>
> Signor: James Patterson

5 May 1877:

> "Catawba Indians located in the eastern portion of York County requesting that William Whyte of Rock Hill be appointed their agent."
>
> Signor: James Patterson

1900 census for Conejos, Sanford County, Colorado:
Household # 95:

Patterson, James……..white…..male…….age: 50….born: SC
Patterson, Elizabeth….white…..female…..age: 50….born: SC
Patterson, Bella……...white……female….age: 24….born: SC
Patterson, James M….white…..male……..age: 13….born: SC
Patterson, Henry A….white…..male……..age: 9……born: Colorado

1910 census for Conejos, Sanford County, Colorado (Special Indian Inquires Addendum):

Household #2:

Patterson, James…Indian…..male…age: 61…..born: SC…Catawba

111

A Wandering Tribe

Patterson, Elizabeth…Indian…female..age: 60…born: SC..Catawba

1920 census for Conejos, Sanford County, Colorado:

Household # 62:

Patterson, James………..Indian…..male………age: 70…..born: SC
Patterson, Elizabeth…….Indian…..female…….age: 70…..born: SC

James G Patterson   **Elizabeth M White**

RED HEAD

The Red Head surname, among the Catawba Indians, is one of only two surnames not introduced by, or adopted from, European settlers (the other being Kegg). The Red Head surname was originally the English version of the Catawba name "Tukahayre" which loosely translated to "tick" or "button." The surname made a series of transformations from "Red Button," "Red Tick," to finally "Red Head," obviously originating from the somatic occurrence of a skin tag.

Tooksesey a.k.a. Billy Red Tick/Red Head (born circa 1720, Catawba Reservation, SC) was a full-blooded Catawba Indian. Billy, along with King Hagler, attended an Albany, New York peace conference in 1771 where the Colonials were attempting to forge a peace treaty between the Catawba and the Cherokee. Billy Red Head went with the Cherokee peace delegation to Echota where the Chiefs of the Cherokee presented him with a string of white beads.

1780:

"Pay bill for Capt Thomas Drennans Company of Catawba Indians":

Signor: Patrick Readhead
Signor: Billey Readhead
"Attached list of those Indians who did service which cannot be vouched for, 1780-1781":
Signor: Capt Redhead

November 24, 1792:

Petition of "the Chief and Head Men of Catawba Nation":

A Wandering Tribe

Signor: Billy Readhead

Patrick Red Head (born circa 1720, Catawba Reservation, SC) was a full-blooded Catawba Indian.

March 28 1793:

Records of Governor Moultrie, South Carolina:

> ....*Whereas I have received information from the Agents appointed to take care of the Rights of the Catawba Indians that a Prosecution has been commenced against several of the said Indians in the Court of the County of Lancaster, to Wit, Patrick Redhead, Jenny Patterson and John Kennedy for trading with Negroes and that it is apprehended that the said Court intends to inflict Corporal Punishment on them. Now know ye that in consideration of the said Indians being Free People and under the protection of this State I do by these Presents pardon and release said Indians from any Judgment or punishment whatever which has been or may be ordered to be inflicted on them by the said Court of which all concerned are to take due Notice and govern themselves accordingly.*

Hand drawn picture of "Captain Red Head" 1771

Red Head

Polly Red Head (born 1809 Catawba Reservation, SC) was among the Catawba who were adopted into the Choctaw Nation, Indian Territory, in 1853.

Sally Red Head (born 1789 Catawba Reservation, SC) was among the Catawba Indians who were living with the Cherokee.

ROBBINS

Effie Harris Robbins (b 1892 Catawba Reservation, SC) was at least ¼ Catawba Indian. She married Frank Robbins, a white man. In the 1930's she and her family moved from Spartanburg, SC back to the Catawba Reservation.

1930 census of Campobello, Spartanburg, SC:

Household # 33:

Robbins, Frank………white……male……….age: 65…….born: SC
Robbins, Effie……..……white……female…….age: 35……born: SC
Robbins, Ester……….white…….female…….age:9……..born: SC
Robbins, George……...white……male….…...age: 5……..born: SC

1940 census of Catawba Township, York County, SC:

Household # 439:

Robbins, Frank……white……male…….age: 75…….born: SC
Robbins, Effie……..Indian…...female…..age: 48……born: SC
Robbins, Ester……..white……female…..age: 20……born: SC
Robbins, Earl………white…...male…….age: 18…….born: SC
Robbins, Flinton…...white…...male…….age: 16…….born: SC
Robbins, Fay……….white…...female…..age: 9……..born: SC

A Wandering Tribe

Family of Frank Robbins & Effie Harris Robbins.

SCOTT

Abraham Scott (born circa 1800 St. Luke's Parish, SC) was at least ½ Indian of unknown tribal origin.

1 Feb 1810:
Affidavit of Betsy Busby of St. Luke's, SC:

> ...*Betsy Busby, being Indian born, the first child born, Nancy Busby likewise, the said Nancy being born an Indian – were exempted from taxes. Therefore, all the children are the same. Children are Lizar Bing, Abraham Scott, Mary Scott, John Brunson, Martha Scott. Witnesses: William Gordon, Edward Saints.*

10 Jan 1845:

Affidavit of Martha DeHay and Ann Beasley of Georgetown, SC:

> ...*Martha DeHay is well acquainted with a free colored woman named Martha Cole, or Scott...She had Abraham Scott as her husband...they are still living together on Charleston neck as husband and wife. She was of Indian descent.*
> *Appeared Ann Beazely...she was well acquainted with Martha Scott, formerly Martha Cole, about 22 years. She had then just come from Camden, SC. She was of Indian descent.*

Isham Scott Sr (born 1763 Catawba Reservation, SC, died 1837 Edgecombe, NC) was at least ½ Catawba Indian, son of Jacob Scott who was "said to be a Chief among the Catawba Indians." Isham Sr married Rebecca Chavers James (widow of Jeremiah James). Isham served in the Revolutionary War, 10th Regiment, North Carolina Continental Line.

Isham Scott Jr (b 1784 Halifax, NC, died after 1870 Calhoun County, FL) was at least ½ Catawba Indian, grandson of Jacob Scott who was "said to be a Chief among the Catawba Indians." He married Margaret Oxendine. After the conclusion of the Revolutionary War, Isham and his wife moved south to Sumter County, SC.

A Wandering Tribe

Isham Scott Jr   Margaret Oxendine
Children:
- John N Scott (b 1804) married Elizabeth Jennings Watts
- James Scott (b 1818) married Mary H (?)
- Eliza "Betsy" Scott (b 1822) married (1st) John Jones (2nd) Joe Quinn (3rd) Francis Hill
- Fleming T Scott (b 1833) married Sarah J Parrott
- Margaret Scott (b 1836) never married.

Isham Scott Jr's wife, Margaret Oxendine Scott, died approximately 1853 and Isham moved south to Calhoun County, Florida, an area that his eldest daughter had journeyed to some ten years earlier.

1863:
Enlistment Roll of "Calhoun Home Guard", Calhoun County, FL:

> .....*Private Isham Scott...5 foot 5 inches...brown eyes...dark hair...dark skin*

1861:
Affidavit of Mary Nickles of Sumter, SC:

> ....*She has known Margaret & Isham Scott the parents of John N Scott and Fleming T Scott for a length of time and that Margaret Scott was a White woman and always had the Character of being White and that Isham Scott's ancestors was of Egyptian and Indian blood.*

1862:
Testimony of Thomas Strickland, Calhoun County, Florida Court case of State V. Francis Hill:

> .....*Knew Isham Scott and Margaret parents of Eliza in Sumter South Carolina. Isham was a man of large amount Indian blood. Margaret was an Oxendine woman of clean complexion nearly white the Indian still apparent. The grandfather, one Jacob, was said to be a Chief among the Catawba Indians.*

Scott

The Scott family, in general, are regarded as free of negro blood.

1862:

Testimony of Francis Hill, Calhoun County, Florida Court case of State V. Francis Hill:

> ...*Only briefly met Isham and Margaret Scott the parents of Eliza. Isham appeared to be mostly Indian. Margaret appeared to be mostly white. Neither appeared to have negro blood or considered Mulatto.*

Eliza Scott Hill   (2nd) **Joseph Quinn**
Children:
- Susan Quinn (born: 1845)
- Delila Quinn (born: 1849)

(3rd) **Francis "Frank" Hill**

Children:
- Marthey Hill (born: 1844) married Daniel Minton
- Ann Hill (born: 1848)
- Joe Hill (born: 1852)
- Quinn Hill (born: 1853)
- Bob Hill (born: 1854)
- Blunt Hill (born: 1856)
- Green Hill (born: 1859)

Dan Minton Jr family
Marthey Hill Minton (seated second from right),
daughter of Eliza Scott Hill

Julia R Minton Hill
Daughter of Marthey Hill Minton

Scott

**Inez Hill family
Descendants of Eliza Scott Hill**

James Scott (born 1753 Halifax NC, died 24 Dec 1826 Sumter, SC) was at least ½ Indian of unknown tribal origin. James married Charity (last name unknown) who was also at least ½ Indian of unknown tribal origin. James served in the Revolutionary War as a private under General Sumter. After the conclusion of the War, James brought his family down from Halifax, NC and settled on the lands of General Sumter.

Jan 1861:

Affidavit of John R Pollard of Sumter, SC:

> ......*I have personal knowledge of James Scott and Charity Scott his wife the grandparents of Michael Oxendine the holder of this certificate and that they came into this county from Virginia when I was very young, and that the said James Scott the grandfather of said Michael Oxendine was a Revolution-*

ary soldier and from and after the passing of the Pension act drew pension money till the day of his death as a revolutionary soldier and that Charity Scott his grandmother was the holder of a certificate certifying that her mother was a clean blooded white woman and that her father was mixed with Indian and their daughter Jane Scott married an Oxendine whom I did not know and that the said Michael Oxendine is the offspring of Jane Scott the wife of Aaron Oxendine and that they lived here and raised a large family of children who always enjoyed their freedom and the general striking physiognomal traits of appearance of the Scott family in general and Relatives is deeply set with European and Indian blood and that there is a number of records in the Clerk's office of Sumter Court house where their Relatives have escaped from under the disabling statute.

James Scott   **Charity (?)**

Children:
- Jane Scott (born 1790) married Aaron Oxendine
- ___daughter___ Scott (born 1793)
- James Scott Jr (born 1795)
- Stephen Scott (born 1798)
- Renty Scott (born 1801)
- Elizabeth Scott (born 1812) married Ferdinand Benenhaley
- Henry Scott (born 1814) married Mary Oxendine
- Catherine Scott (born 1815) married Joseph Benenhaley Jr.

John Scott (born Halifax, NC) was at least ½ Indian of unknown tribal origin. He married Peggy (last name unknown) who was a full-blooded Indian of unknown tribal origin.

August 1896:

Scott

Affidavit of James J King of Halifax, NC:

> *...states that he is a resident of Halifax County and are 95 years of age and that he is well acquainted with the ancestors of Elijah and Dock Evans, that his grandmother Peggy Scott was an Indian and his grandfather John Scott had Indian blood in him and they were the mother and father of Leven Evans and Harriet Evans who was the mother and father of Elijah and Dock Evans.*

August 1896:

Affidavit of William Stokes of Halifax, NC:

> *...that he is a resident of Halifax County and that he is 81 years of age and that he is personally acquainted with Elijah Evins and Dock Evins and their ancestors Leven Evins and Harriet Evins their father and mother and John Scott and Peggy Scott their Grandfather, and mother. John Scott was the father of Harriet Evens and Peggy Scott was her mother and Elijah and Dock Evens is the sons of Harriet Evens and the grandsons of John Scott who was said to have Indian blood in him, and Peggy Scott was the grandmother of the said Elijah and Dock Evins and the said Peggy Scott was an Indian of the Cherokee Tribe.*

Martha Francis Scott (born circa 1790 Catawba Reservation, SC) was a full-blooded Catawba Indian. She married John Latty and removed to Indian Territory.

June 1879 Tahlequah, Oklahoma:

Statement of Francis Latta before J.A. Sialis, Clerk, on behalf of the Cherokee citizenship claim of Benjamin Brackett:

A Wandering Tribe

....I am a Catawba by blood. My father was also. I was born in North Carolina near the Catawba lands. The Catawba lands may have join both North & South Carolina. I do not speak the Cherokee Language. I do understand it much. I knew John Wilkerson's Mother. She lived near Macker Jack Cove. Her name was Mollie. Claimed white and Cherokee blood. During the Revolution War John Wilkerson's father went to ninety-six South Carolina and afterward his wife went down and they remained there until their children were grown. Two of whom there married. I neither knew claimant, his father or mother. Old man Wilkerson got mad with the widow and had her house burned. He and the widow's sister were going to be married. [illegible] married a man named Hubbard. The other of Nellie Wilkerson I suppose was a white woman. Hubbard I suppose was a white man. Signed: J.A. Sialis, Clerk Note: Francis is Martha Frances Latty nee Scott borned abt 1790 married John Latty borned 1758.

SIZEMORE

Edward "Old Ned" Sizemore (born prior to 1725) was at least a half-blooded Indian of unknown origin, and lived in Lunenburg, Virginia in the 1740's, then was living on the Catawba reservation in the 1750's with the family of James Hart. Sizemore moved to Georgia in the 1760's to be eligible to receive a 150-acre land grant, which he quickly sold and moved back alongside James Hart, who had by then relocated to Wilkes County, North Carolina. Old Ned and James Hart, along with Ned's three eldest sons, Edward, George, and Owen, were all staunch Tories during the Revolutionary War. Old Ned "the Tory Sizemore" was hung by Col. Benjamin Cleveland in Wilkesboro, North Carolina in 1780.

Almost all of the descendants of "Old Ned" Sizemore applied to be included in the Guion Miller Cherokee enrollment of the early 1900's. The majority of descendants claimed that "Old Ned" was a "Full blooded Cherokee," however they were unable to produce any evidence that Old Ned had ever had any connection to the Cherokee Nation, and thus all their claims were rejected as Miller believed them to be "connected to the Catawba Tribe." Afterwards, Frank Sizemore, one of the hundreds of claimants, wrote a personal letter of appeal:

"Mr. Guion Miller, the Sizemores of old man Ned was the people that was actually entitled to that money tho we all got our blanks wrong. We claimed through his descent and we ought to have claimed through her descent. We all failed to give her Indian name and it was Aruna Hart...He married this squaw woman...Ed Sizemore was his name and Elizabeth Hart, if mistaken not, was her name." Frank is obviously referring to Annie "Aruna" Elizabeth Hart, the daughter of James Hart and wife of George Sizemore son of Edward "Old Ned" Sizemore.

Modern use of DNA testing has allowed Sizemore descendants further evidence to reinforce many of the statements made in these early-

A Wandering Tribe

1900's applications. YDNA testing of the family have revealed that the Sizemores do indeed originate from a Native American male progenitor, so either "Old Ned" Sizemore or his father was undoubtedly a full-blooded Indian.

George "All Chief" Sizemore (born 1750, Catawba Reservation, SC) was the son of Edward "Old Ned" Sizemore and Elizabeth Jackson. He married Annie "Aruna" Elizabeth Hart. He and Annie lived in North Carolina, Tennessee, and eventually Kentucky, where George died in 1822. His children and grandchildren in Kentucky began calling him "Chief of All" or "All Chief" because "all of the Kentucky Sizemores descend from him."

Annie "Aruna" Elizabeth Hart Sizemore (born circa 1750, Catawba Reservation, SC) was at least half-blooded Catawba Indian, a daughter of James Hart. She married George Sizemore in Wilkes County, North Carolina circa 1770.

**George "All Chief" Sizemore
and Annie "Aruna" Elizabeth Hart Sizemore**

Sizemore

George Sizemore   **Annie "Aruna" Hart**

Children:

- Catherine "Dolly" Sizemore (born 1770) married James Hart
- John "Rock House" Sizemore (born 1771)
- Winnifred Minerva Sizemore (born 1772) married William T Begley
- Lydia Sizemore (born 1775) married James Blevins
- Sarah "Sallie" Sizemore (born 1776) married Elias Osborne
- George "Golden Hawk" Sizemore (b 1783)
- Edward B "Ned" Sizemore (born 1788) married Annie Baldwin
- Rhoda Sizemore (born 1789) married Aaron Brock
- Henry "Hunting Shirt" Sizemore (born 1790)
- Owen Sizemore (born 1793) married Rebecca Anderson
- Reverend George J Sizemore (born 1797) married Jennie Baldwin

April 1908

Deposition of W.H. Blevins of Kentucky to Guion Miller:

> *……..I remember one Elisha Blevins, who said that Old Ned Sizemore came from the Catawba river, or the Catawba Reservation, as he called it…In 1896, we wanted to go to the Indian Territory, and organized for that purpose. When the band was first organized, there were about 2,175, I believe. They were all Sizemore descendants.*

A Wandering Tribe

Russell Sizemore **Sarah Sizemore**

STEPHENS

Alexander Harris Stephens (born 1829 Jackson County, FL) married Matilda Scott.

Alexander H Stephens	Matilda Scott

Children:
- Edwin Stephens (born: 1859 FL)
- Gideon E Stephens (born: 1861 FL)
- George W Stephens (born: 1863 FL) married Dicie "Lizzie" Godwin – moved to Escambia Co, FL
- Susan M Stephens (born: 1865 FL)

1864:

Enlistment Roll of the 2nd Florida Calvary Company A (Union):

> *Private Alexander H. Stephens…born 1829 in Jackson County [Florida]…5 foot 10 inches…dark brown eyes…dark hair…dark skin…died of disease late 1865.*

1850 census of Calhoun County, Florida:

Household # 66:

Scott, Abslom…….mulatto……..male…….age: 60….born: NC
Scott, Gillatia……...white……….female…..age: 38….born: NC
Scott, Jacob……….mulatto……..male…….age: 17….born: GA
Scott, Amanda…….mulatto…….female…...age:14….born: GA
Scott, Mary Ann…...mulatto…….female…..age: 11….born: GA
Scott, John T……….mulatto…….male……..age: 9…...born: GA
Scott, Samuel……...mulatto…….male……..age: 5…...born: FL
Scott, Henry………..mulatto…….male…….age: 2…...born: FL

Stephens, Alexander.mulatto.......male......age: 20.....born: FL

Thomas Stephens (born 1830 according to his Mormon baptism record in Charleston, SC) was a full-blooded Catawba Indian. He died 14 Dec 1905 after freezing to death while trying to visit his wife's grave in Lancaster, SC.

Polly Stephens (born 1825 Catawba Reservation, SC) was a full-blooded Catawba Indian.

1854:
Report to the Governor of South Carolina on the Catawba Indian by Agent B.S. Massey:

> *"Tom and Polly Stephens, left for Charleston in 1851."*
> *[note: Tom Stephens had returned to the Catawba Reservation by 1863.]*

11 Oct 1863:

Petition of Catawba Indians:
Signed: Tom Stevens

1870 census of St. Luke's Parish, Beaufort County, SC:

Household # 1018:

Stevens, John..."In" marked thru with "M"...male..age: 48..born: SC
Stevens, Rebecca....mulatto
Jr........................... mulatto....male......age: 16......born: SC
Stevens, Elizabeth..mulatto...female....age: 14.......born: SC
Stevens, Mary.......mulatto...female....age: 9.......born: SC

Stephens

Stevens, Martha…..mulatto…….female….age: 6…born: SC
Stevens, Rebecca…mulatto…….female….age: 3…born: SC
Stevens, Julia……..mulatto…….female….age: 1…born: SC

TAYLOR

Atteke a.k.a. Captain Tom Taylor (born circa 1720 SC) was a full-blooded Catawba Indian. Tom was among the Catawba Indians called into service to catch runaway slaves after the Stone River slave insurrection in 1739. He received Indian commissions from Lt. Governor William Bull in 1740 and 1741.

Richard L Taylor (born 1781 North Carolina) was at least ½ Catawba Indian. He married Susannah Chavers.

In September, 1853, a band of 18 Indians, all of whom claimed to be Catawba, was reported by Brigadier General G.B. Hall as wandering near Stockton, Alabama (near present-day Atmore, Alabama). Their leader was named Taylor and there were four men in the group; the rest were women and children. They said they came from northwest Florida, and were enroute to Arkansas, but were stranded for lack of money and had been begging corn and potatoes in Alabama where residents were anxious to get rid of them.

[Records of the Bureau of Indian Affairs, National Archives, Letters

A Wandering Tribe

Received, Miscellaneous, 1853, A-172, Brig.-Gen. G.B. Hall to Capt. I.C. Casey about Certain Indians in his County, November 12, 1853]

1850 census of 3rd Division, Walton County, Florida:

Household # 207:

Taylor, Richard…….white……male……age: 71……..born: NC
Taylor, Susanah……white……female….age: 34……..born: GA
Taylor, Jacob………white……male…….age:12……..born: FL
Taylor, Martha……..white……female…..age: 10…….born: FL
Taylor, James………white……male…….age: 7……..born: FL
Taylor, Margaret……white…...female…..age: 4……..born: FL
Taylor, William……..white…...male…….age: 2……..born: FL
Taylor, David………white…….male…….age: 9……..born: FL

Household # 208:

Chavers, Ann………white……female…..age: 39…..born: GA
Chavers, Clabourn…white……female…..age: 19…..born: ALA
Chavers, Luiza……..white…….female…age: 17…...born: ALA
Chavers, Mary……..white…….female…age: 11…..born: ALA
Chavers, Charity……white…….female…age: 9…….born: FL
Chavers, Nancy……..white…….female…age: 7…….born: FL
Chavers, William……white…….male…...age: 1……born: FL

We know that there were 11 individuals in the family of Richard Taylor between the 1850 and 1860 censuses (Richard, Susannah, Jacob, Martha, James, Margaret, William, John D, Susannah, Elizabeth, and Millia), then by adding the 7 who were recorded in the household of Ann Chavers (Ann, Claiborne, Louisa, Mary, Charity, Nancy, and William) we have the total of 18 "Catawba Indians" mentioned in the report. Richard Taylor, Jacob Taylor, James Taylor, and Calbourn

Taylor

Chavers were of appropriate age to be described as the "four men in the group."

In agreement with the 1853 report, we find the family of Richard L Taylor living near Atmore in 1860 recorded as an "Indian" family:

1860 census of Baldwin County, Alabama:

Household # 381:

Taylor, R L……….Indian……….male……...age: 79……...born: NC
Taylor, Susanah….Indian……..female…….age: 45……...born: GA
Taylor, Jacob……..Indian……..male……...age: 23……...born: ALA
Taylor, James…….Indian……..male……...age: 16……...born: ALA
Taylor, Margaret…Indian……..female…….age: 14……...born: FL
Taylor, William…..Indian……..male……...age: 11……...born: FL
Taylor, Susanah…..Indian……..female……..age: 9……...born: FL
Taylor, Elizabeth…Indian……..female……..age: 6……..born: ALA
Taylor, Milly……..Indian……..female…..…age: 3……...born: ALA

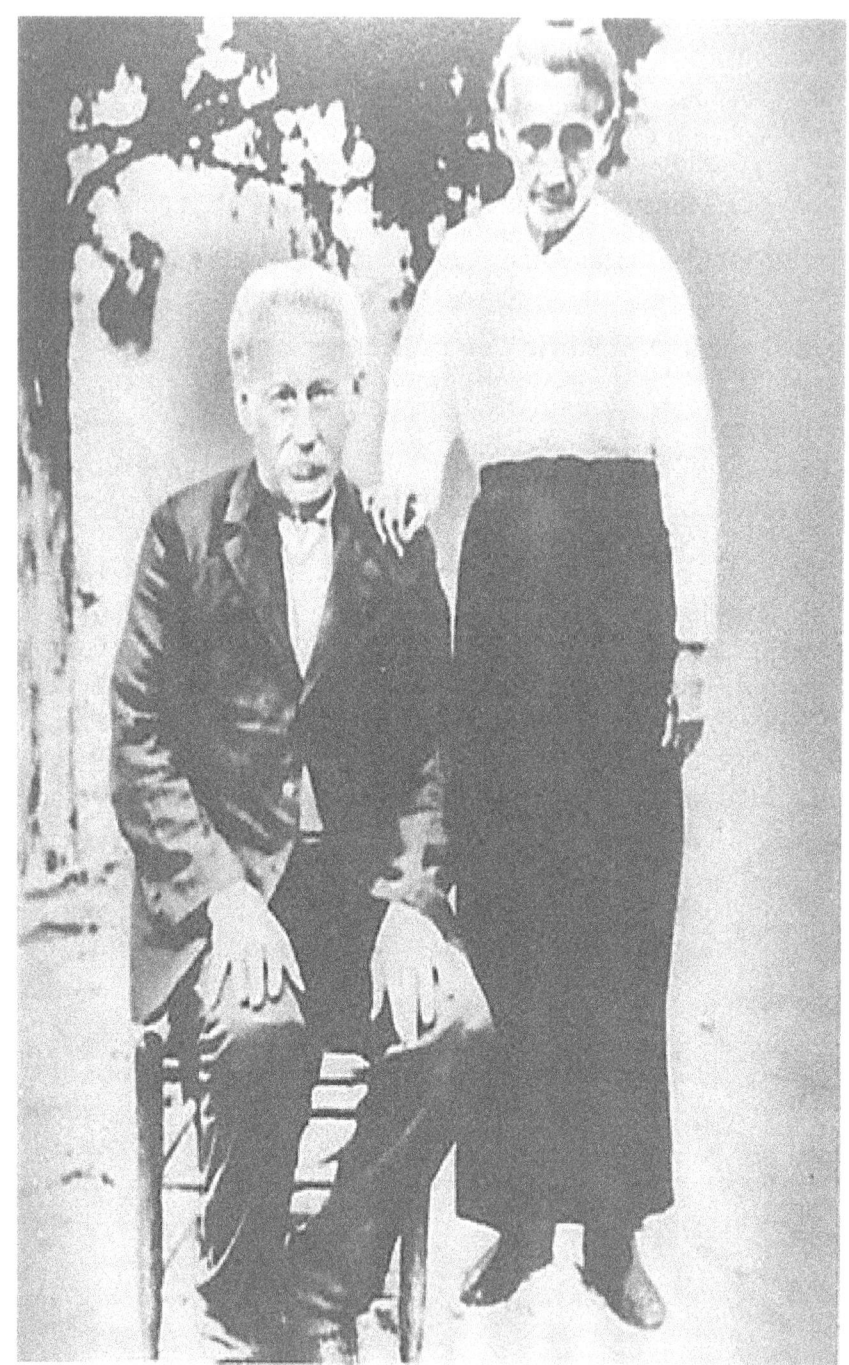

Elizabeth Taylor (daughter of Richard L and Susannah Taylor) and her husband, John Alexander.

Taylor

By 1870 Richard had left Alabama and returned to Florida.

1870 census of Pensacola P.O., Escambia County, Florida:

Household # 105:

Taylor, Richard.......white.......male.......age: 90......born: NC
Taylor, Susanna......white.......female.....age: 53.......born: GA
Taylor, William......white........male.......age: 21......born: FL
Taylor, Susanna........white......female......age: 17......born: FL
Taylor, Elizabeth......white......female......age: 15......born: ALA
Taylor, Millie.........white......female......age: 12......born: FL

1880 census of Vill of Molina, Escambia County, Florida:

Household # 267:

Taylor, Richard......white.......male......age: 89.......born: NC
Taylor, Susan........white.......female....age: 64.......born: GA
Taylor, Mattie.......white.......female....age: 4.........born: FL

Richard L Taylor died in Escambia County, FL in 1884 and was buried in Lathran Chapel Cemetery.

Richard L Taylor	**Susannah Chavers**
Born: 1781 North Carolina	born: 1817 Georgia
Died: 1884 Escambia County, FL	died: Escambia County, FL

Children:
- Jacob C Taylor (born 1838 Coffee County, Alabama) married Melissa Kimbrough 06 Apr 1871.
- Martha Taylor (born 1840 Coffee County, Alabama) dead by 1860.
- John D Taylor (born 1841 Coffee County, Alabama) married Manerva Payne 23 Aug 1868.

A Wandering Tribe

- James R Taylor (born 1843 Coffee County, Alabama) married Sarah (?).
- Margaret Taylor (born 1846 Walton County, FL) killed by lightning in 1862.
- William H Taylor (born 1848 Walton County, FL) married Margie A Smith 29 Dec 1872.
- Susannah Taylor (born 1851 Walton County, FL) married Hiram Kimbrough 21 Nov 1871.
- Elizabeth Taylor (born 1854 Baldwin County, Alabama) married John Alexander 28 may 1875.
- Millie Taylor (born 1857 Baldwin County, Alabama) married Alvin Alexander 06 Oct 1878.

1880 census of Holmans, Baldwin County, Alabama:

Unmarked household:

Taylor, Jacob..........Indian...male..........age: 48........born: FL
Taylor, Melissa......white....female.........age: 24........born: GA
Taylor, Jacob..........white.....male..........age: 7..........born: FL
Taylor, Susan..........white....female........age: 5..........born: FL
Taylor, Margaret......white...female........age: 3..........born: FL
Taylor, Andrew P......white...male..........age: 1..........born: FL

Unmarked Household:

Taylor, William H.......Indian...male......age: 28.......born: FL
Taylor, Margie Ann......white...female.....age: 25.......born: FL
Taylor, Henry.............white....male......age: 7........born: FL
Taylor, Charles...........white...male.......age: 4........born: FL
Taylor, James..............white...male.......age: 2.......born: FL

Taylor

John Daniel Taylor and his wife, Manerva Payne

A Wandering Tribe

1880 census of Hinds County, Mississippi:

Household # 27:

Taylor, John............mulatto......male......age: 31...born: MS
Taylor, Minerva........black.........female....age: 27...born: GA
Taylor, Emma..........black.........female.....age: 9....born: MS
Taylor, Martha.........black..........female.....age: 6....born: MS
Taylor, John............black..........male.......age: 3.....born: MS
Taylor, Francis.........black.........female.....age: 1.....born: MS

1900 census of Hinds County, Mississippi:

Household # 286:

Taylor, John.........black......male.........age: 55........born: ALA
Taylor, Minerva.....black......female......age: 51........born: GA
Taylor, John.........black......male.........age: 23........born: MS
Taylor, Hilliard......black......male.........age: 15........born: MS
Taylor, Willie.......black......male.........age: 14........born: MS
Taylor, Gideon......black......male.........age: 10........born: MS
Taylor, Andrew......black......male.........age: 7..........born: MS
Taylor, Austin.......black......male.........age: 4..........born: MS
Taylor, Clinton......black......male.........age: 2..........born: MS

1910 census of Harrison County, Mississippi:

Household # 104:

Taylor, John D.........white........male.......age: 68..........born: FL
Taylor, Minerva........white........female.......age: 57.......born: AL
Taylor, Lander..........white........male.......age: 17..........born: AL
Taylor, Walter..........white........male.......age: 15..........born: AL
Martin, Anna............white........female.......age: 20.......born: LA

TIMS

John Alexander Tims (born July 1845, Catawba Reservation, SC) was a half-blooded Catawba Indian, son of Rachel Mursh, who was half Catawba and half Pamunkey Indian. John first married Martha Ann Scott, a half-blooded Catawba (daughter of Betsy Mursh Scott and a white man).

J Alexander Tims' second marriage (after 1900) was to Sarah Evans Canty Head (born 1 July 1845 Catawba Reservation, SC) a full-blooded Catawba, daughter of Chancy Evans and Peggy Canty, and widow of Robert Henry Head.

1860 census for York County, SC:

Household # 518:

Watts, Evans……..white…….male……….age: 49……..born: SC
Watts, Lucy………..white……female…….age: 40……..born: SC
Head, Robert H…..white…….male………..age: 18……..born: SC
Head, Emily Eliz…white……female…….age: 16……..born: SC
Head, Peggy Jane…white…...female…….age:14……...born: SC
Head, John R……..white……male………..age: 12……..born: SC
Watts, Nancy C…..white……female……...age: 5………..born: SC
Watts, James H…...white……male………..age: 2………...born: SC
Watts, W D………..white……male………...age: 1………...born: SC
Timms, John L…....white…....male……….age: 14……..born: SC

Catawba Indian petition of 5 May 1877

> "Catawba Indians located in the eastern portion of York County requesting that William Whyte of Rock Hill be appointed their agent.":
>
> *Signed: A. Tims, Chief*

A Wandering Tribe

1880 census Catawba, York County, SC:

Household # 312:
Tims, Alex..........Indian......male......age: 40..............born: SC
Tims, Ann...........Indian......female...age: 35..............born: SC
Tims, Rachel........Indian......female...age: 14..............born: SC
Tims, Harry.........Indian......male......age: 12..............born: SC

1900 census Conejos, Sanford County, Colorado:

Household # 4:

Tims, Alexander.........white.......male......age: 54.........born: SC
Tims, Martha A..........white.......female....age: 52.........born: NC
Tims, Robert H..........white.......male......age: 22.........born: SC
Harris, Rachel.............white.......female...age: 34..........born: SC
Harris, Alexander..........white.......male......age: 12..........born: SC
Harris, Eveline............white.......female...age: 9...........born: SC
Harris, Ellis................white.......male......age: 7..........born: Tex

1930 census San Juan County, New Mexico:
Household # 9:

Tims, Alexander...male.......white.......age: 84..............born: SC
Harris, Rachel......female....white.......age: 63..............born: SC

1940 census Fruitland, San Juan County, New Mexico:
Household # 62:
Tims, J. Alexander...male.......white.......age: 94......born: SC
Harris, Rachel.........female....white.......age: 74......born: SC

Tims

John Alexander Tims
1845-1941

A Wandering Tribe

**Sarah Evans Canty Tims
1845-1919**

TYLER

Priss Tyler (born circa 1718 Catawba Reservation, SC) was a full blooded Catawba Indian.

1769 & 1771:

Petitions for Release From Servitude, Louisa County, VA:

> *Priss Tyler....a Catawba Indian who was induced by an Indian trader named Captain Robert Hicks to come to Virginia with him in about 1733. Hicks sold her into slavery. Her children to wit: Joseph Tyler, Nan Tyler, Betty Tyler, Priss Tyler, Bartlett Tyler*

George Tyler
Son of John Tyler & Mary Guy

WATTS

Lucy (?) Cobb Watts (born Nov 1818, Catawba Reservation, SC) was a full-blooded Catawba Indian.

Lucy first married John Cobbs before 1850, then married Evans Watts before 1860.

1850 census for York County, SC:

Household # 1049:

Cobb, John.........white.......male..........age: 35.......born: SC
Cobb, Lucinda......white......female........age: 30........born: SC
Cobb, Mary.........white......female.......age: 6.........born: SC
Cobb, Martha.......white......female.......age:3..........born: SC
Cobb, Elizabeth.....white.....female........age:1..........born: SC
Cobb, Martha........white.....female........age: 64.......born: VA

1860 census for York County, SC:

Household # 518:

Watts, Evans......white........male..........age: 49.......born: SC
Watts, Lucy........white.......female........age: 40......born: SC
Head, Robert H.....white.......male..........age: 18......born: SC
Head, Emily Eliz...white......female.......age: 16.......born: SC
Head, Peggy Jane...white......female.......age:14.......born: SC
Head, John R.........white.....male.........age: 12.......born: SC
Watts, Nancy C......white......female.......age: 5.........born: SC
Watts, James H......white......male.........age: 2.........born: SC
Watts, W D............white......male........age: 1.........born: SC
Timms, John L........white......male.........age: 14.......born: SC

Catawba Indian petition of 1863: To SC Legislature regarding Indian Agent to the Catawba J.R. Patton:

A Wandering Tribe

Signer: Lucy Watts

1880 census for Steel Creek, Mecklenburg County, NC:

Household # 212:

Watts, Iven……..white…….male…………..age: 64……....born: SC
Watts, Lucy……...Indian…....female……....age: 62……....born: SC
Watts, Nancy C….Indian…..female……....age: 35……....born: SC
Watts, James…….Indian…..male…………..age: 22……....born: SC
Watts, William D..Indian…...male…………..age:20……....born: SC
Watts, Mary J……Indian…...female……....age: 24……....born: SC
Watts, Elizabeth…Indian…..female……....age: 5……....born: SC
Chapen, Alex…….white…....male…………..age: 12…….born: NC

1880 census for Harmony, Washington County, Utah:

Household # 190:

Watts, William D……white…male…….age: 30…….born: SC
Watts, Nancy………..white…female…..age: 10…….born: SC
Watts, Henry J………white…male…….age: 35…….born: SC
Watts, Laura L……….white…female…..age: 22…….born: SC
Watts, Kattie H……….white…female…..age:20…….born: Utah
Watts, Annie M……...white…female…...age: 24……born: Utah
Watts, Vory W………..white….male……..age: 5……born: Utah

Household # 191:

Watts, Evans………..white…...male…………age: 83……....born: SC
Watts, Lucy………....white…...female……..age: 81……….born: SC

146

Watts

William D Watts
1860-1933

Appendix 1

BEAUFORT DISTRICT INDIAN SETTLEMENT

1790 Census Beaufort District:

Alexander Brown.......1 Free Person of Color
Sarah Gibbs..............4 Free Persons of Color
John Bing................5 Free Persons of Color
Matthew Bing............5 Free Persons of Color
Mary Buzby..............1 Free Person of Color
John Evans...............2 Free Persons of Color
William Gordon.......7 Free persons of Color...1 Slave
[see Busby Affidavit of 1 Feb 1810]
David Howard...........4 Free Persons of Color
James Howard...........3 Free Persons of Color
Richard Jones............8 Free Persons of Color
William Jones...........8 Free Persons of Color
Moses Scott..............8 Free Persons of Color

1850 census of Saint Luke's Parish of Beaufort District, SC:

Household # 270:

Newton, Robert.........mulatto....male......age: 38.........born: SC
Newton, Ann............mulatto....female....age: 35.........born: SC

Household # 272:

Williams, Stephen...black......male.......age: 55......born: SC
Williams, Ann........black......female....age: 40......born: SC
Williams, Elizabeth...black......female.....age: 8.......born: SC
Williams, Harriet.....black.....female.....age: 6........born: SC

A Wandering Tribe

Williams, Sarah A…black……..female…..age: 4……..born: SC
Williams, Milly A…black…….female…..age: 3……..born: SC
Williams, George….black……..male……age: 1……..born: SC

Household # 273:

Scott, Charles………mulatto….male…..age: 27……..born: SC
Scott, Amelia……….mulatto….female…..age: 30…....born: SC
Scott, Charlotte……..mulatto….female…..age: 7…….born: SC
Scott, Charles……….mulatto….male…..age: 4………born: SC
Williams, Thomas…..mulatto….male…..age: 14……..born: SC
Jones, F……………...mulatto….male…..age: 12……..born: SC

Household # 274:

Mims, John………….black……..male…….age: 40…....born: SC
Mims, Isabella……...mulatto…..female…..age: 30…....born: SC
Mims, Annie………..mulatto…..female…..age: 16…....born: SC
Mims, John………….mulatto…..male……..age: 10…....born: SC
Mims, Amanda……..mulatto…..female …..age: 7…….born: SC
Mims, Agnes………..mulatto…..female…..age:5……..born: SC
Mims, Alfred………..mulatto…..male…….age: 2…….born: SC

Household # 275:

Harvey, William……...mulatto…..male…….age: 50….born: SC
Harvey, Rachel……......mulatto….female…..age: 55…..born:SC
Harvey, George Anna…mulatto….female…..age: 16…..born: SC
Bing, Sarah…………….mulatto…..female….age: 75…..born: SC

Household # 276:

Newton, Edward……mulatto……male…...age: 26……born: SC
Newton, Kizia………mulatto……female....age: 25……born: SC
Newton, Louiver……mulatto……male…...age: 3……..born: SC
Newton, Kizia………mulatto……female....age: 1……..born: SC

Household # 277:

Appendix 1

Busby, Jessie………..mulatto…….male……...age: 31….born: SC
Busby, Celia…………..mulatto…….female…..age: 26….born: SC
Busby, Delia…………..mulatto…….female…..age: 9…...born: SC
Busby, Elizabeth……...mulatto…….female…..age: 1…..born: SC

Household # 278:

Busby, Jerry…………..mulatto…….male……...age: 28…..born: SC
Busby, Betsy…………..mulatto…….female…...age: 35…..born: SC
Busby, Ann…………...mulatto……female……age: 4…...born: SC
Busby, Lawrence……..mulatto…….male……...age: 2…...born: SC
Busby, Jeridiah……….mulatto…….male……...age: 1…...born: SC

Household # 279:

Busby, Amos………..mulatto…….male……...age: 40…..born: SC
Busby, Annie………..mulatto…….female…...age: 20…..born: SC
Busby, Mary………...mulatto…….female…...age: 3….....born: SC

Household # 280:

Busby, Isham………..mulatto…….male……...age: 65…...born: SC
Busby, Mary…………black………female…...age: 60…...born: SC
Busby, Ulysses……...black………..male……...age:22…...born: SC
Busby, Fanny………..black……….female…..age: 17…..born: SC

Household # 281:

Railsford, Edward……mulatto…...male…….age: 75…….born: SC
Railsford, Louisa……..black……..female…..age: 50…….born: SC
Scott, Sarah…………...black……..female…...age: 10……born: SC
Busby, Catherine……..black……..female…...age: 6……..born: SC

Household # 282:

Henson, Henry……….mulatto……..male……age: 22…...born: SC
Henson, Mary………..mulatto……..female…..age: 20…..born: SC
Jones, Eugenia……….mulatto……..female…...age: 3…...born: SC

A Wandering Tribe

Household # 283:

Jones, James………mulatto……male………age: 27…..born: SC
Jones, Catherine…..mulatto……female…….age: 24…..born: SC
Newton, Virginia….mulatto……female…….age: 8……born: SC
Jones, Artimis……..mulatto……female…….age: 4…….born: SC
Jones, Toyansilla….mulatto……female…….age: 2……born: SC

Household # 284:

Morrison, James…mulatto…male…age: 40..born: SC [Catawba Indian]
Morrison, Sarah….mulatto…female….age: 40…..born: SC
Morrison, James…mulatto….male……age: 17….born: SC

Household # 285:

McKinley, Archibald…mulatto…male……age: 30….born: SC
McKinley, Sarah……...mulatto…female….age: 26….born: SC
McKinley, Mary……...mulatto…female…..age: 6…...born: SC
McKinley, Archibald…mulatto…female….age: 4…...born: SC
McKinley, Valeria……mulatto…female….age: 2……born: SC
Morrison, J…………..mulatto…male……age: 1……born: SC

Household # 286:

Scott, Thomas……….mulatto……male……age: 25….born: SC
Scott, Betsy…………mulatto……female….age: 21…..born: SC
Scott, Moses………...mulatto……male…....age: 13…..born: SC

Household # 289:

Bing, Mathew………mulatto……male…..age: 47…...born: SC
Bing, Caroline……...mulatto……female…age: 43…...born: SC
Bing, Elizabeth……..mulatto……female…age: 16…...born: SC
Bing, Julius…………mulatto…….male……age: 15….born: SC
Bing, Selina………...mulatto……female…age: 12…..born: SC
Bing, Lisbon………..mulatto……male…...age: 10…..born: SC
Bing, Laura…………mulatto……female…age: 8……born: SC

Appendix 1

Bing, Mary…………..mulatto……female…age: 6……..born: SC
Bing, Joel M………….mulatto……male…..age: 1……born: SC

Household # 290:

Jones, Thomas….mulatto………male…….age: 25…….born: SC
Jones, Susan…….mulatto………female…..age: 20……born: SC
Jones, George…...mulatto………male…….age: 5……..born: SC
Jones, Ann………mulatto………female…..age: 4……..born: SC
Jones, Sarah……..mulatto………female…..age: 1……..born: SC

Household # 291:

Bing, Francis……mulatto…male……age: 24……born: SC
Bing, Martha……mulatto…female….age: 20……born: SC
Bing. Betsy……...black……female…age: 60…….born: SC
[see Bing Affidavit of 10 Feb 1827]

Household # 292:

Bing, James………mulatto……male……age: 22…born: SC
Bing, Harriet……..black………female….age: 20….born: SC

Household # 293:

Jenkins, James……white………male……age: 65…born: England
Jenkins, Louisa……black……...female….age: 55…born: SC

Household # 294:

Jenkins, James……mulatto……male……age: 25……born: SC
Jenkins, Louisa…...mulatto……female….age: 25……born: SC
Jenkins, Thirsa……mulatto……female….age: 25……born: SC
Jenkins, Sarah…….mulatto……female….age: 25……born: SC
Jenkins, Timothy....mulatto……male……age: 25……born: SC

Household # 295:

Jenkins, Charles……mulatto……male……age: 22……born: SC

153

A Wandering Tribe

Jenkins, Miley………mulatto……female….age: 20……born: SC
Jenkins, Mynerva…..mulatto……female….age: 1……..born: SC

Household # 296:

Scott, Ann………..mulatto……female…..age: 46….born: SC
Scott, Martha……mulatto……female…..age: 15…..born: SC
Scott, Elijah……..mulatto……female…..age: 12…..born: SC
Scott, Ann………..mulatto……female…..age: 9……born: SC
Scott, Margaret….mulatto……female…..age: 6……born: SC
Scott, Mary………mulatto…...female…..age: 1……born: SC

Household # 297:

Jones, Westley……mulatto……male……age: 26……born: SC
Jones, Mary Ann….mulatto……female….age: 19……born: SC

Household # 298:

Jones, William………mulatto……male……age: 60…….born: SC
Jones, Rachel………..mulatto…...female….age: 30…….born: SC
Jones, Jane…………..mulatto…...female….age: 11…….born: SC

Household # 299:

Jenkins, Thomas…mulatto……male……age: 27…….born: SC
Jenkins, Elsy……..mulatto……female….age: 28…….born: SC
Jenkins, Jim……...mulatto……male…….age: 7……..born: SC
Jenkins, Hampton…mulatto…..male…….age: 3……..born: SC
Jenkins, Margaret…mulatto…..female…..age: 1……..born: SC

Household # 300:

Henson, James……mulatto……male………age: 22………..born: SC
Henson, Martha…..mulatto……female…….age: 20………..born: SC
Henson, Maner……mulatto……male………age: 4…………..born: SC

Household # 301:

Appendix 1

Newton, Joseph......mulatto......male.......age: 22...........born: SC
Newton, Elizah.......black.........female......age: 20..........born: SC
Scott, Catherine......mulatto......female......age: 7............born: SC

Household # 302:

Jones, David.......black.........male......age: 40.......born: SC
Jones, Rebecca....mulatto.......female...age: 35........born: SC
Jones, Willis.......black.........male......age: 13.......born: SC
Jones, Westley... .black ....male......age: 11......born: SC
Jones, Misouriah...black ....female...age: 8........born: SC
Jones, Francis......black ....male.......age: 7.........born: SC
Jones, Frederick...black..........male......age: 6........born: SC
Jones, Hardee......black ....male......age: 4.......born: SC
Jones, Barney......black ....male......age: 1.......born: SC

Household # 303:

Jones, Cornelius......mulatto.......male......age: 35......born: SC
Jones, Jane.............mulatto......female....age: 27......born: SC
Jones, Jenette.........mulatto......female....age: 15......born: SC
Jones, Margaret.......mulatto......female....age: 13.......born: SC
Jones, Irvin.............mulatto......male......age: 11......born: SC
Jones, Albert..........mulatto.......male......age: 9.......born: SC
Jones, Ferman.........mulatto......male.......age: 4.......born: SC
Jones, Allison..........mulatto.......male......age: 2.......born: SC

Household # 304:

Bing, Washington......mulatto......female......age: 26....born: SC
Bing, Harriet............mulatto......female.....age: 25.....born: SC
Bing, Jane...............mulatto.......female....age: 1.......born: SC
Bing, Oliver............mulatto........male......age: 10......born: SC

Household # 305:

Gordon, David......mulatto.........male......age: 45.......born: SC
Gordon, Eliza [Bing].....mulatto...female....age: 45.......born: SC
[Busby Affidavit of 1 Feb 1810]

Gordon, Charles..........mulatto...male.......age: 21......born: SC
Gordon, Joshua...........mulatto...male........age: 20......born: SC
Gordon, William..........mulatto...male........age: 14......born: SC
Gordon, Isaac ["Stell"]mulatto.......male......age: 14......born: SC
[married Lucinda Harris]
Gordon, Sarah...........mulatto.......female....age: 38....born: SC
Gordon, Selina..........mulatto.......female.....age: 6.....born: SC
Gordon, David..........mulatto........male......age: 35....born: SC
Gordon, Elias............mulatto.......male......age: 35....born: SC

Household # 306:

Jones, Richard......mulatto......male......age: 52......born: SC
Jones, Charity.......mulatto......female....age: 55......born: SC
Jones, Ulysses.......mulatto......male......age: 23......born: SC
Jones, Patrick........mulatto.......male......age: 21......born: SC
Jones, Naomi.........mulatto......female....age: 19.......born: SC

Household # 307:

Padgett, John.......mulatto......male......age: 36......born: SC
Padgett, Elizabeth..mulatto......female.....age: 35......born: SC
Padgett, Annie......mulatto......female.....age: 28......born: SC
Padgett, Mary.......mulatto......female.....age: 8........born: SC
Padgett, Emma......mulatto......female......age: 6.......born: SC
Beckett, Ann.........mulatto......female.....age: 25......born: SC

Household # 308:

Jackson, Richard...mulatto......male......age: 35.......born: SC
Jackson, Caroline...mulatto......female....age: 30......born: SC
Jackson, James......mulatto........male......age: 12......born: SC
Jackson, Mary......mulatto.......female....age: 8........born: SC
Jackson, John........mulatto.......male.....age: 6.........born: SC
Jackson, Martha.....mulatto.......female...age: 4.........born: SC
Jackson, Maria......mulatto.......female....age: 1........born: SC

Household # 309

Appendix 1

Martin, Caroline…..mulatto……female……age: 30…..born: SC

Household # 310:

Simmons, Rebecca…mulatto……female…age: 35……born: SC
Simmons, Sarah…….mulatto…...female….age: 10…....born: SC
Simmons, Molly……mulatto…...female….age: 2……..born: SC

1860 census of Saint Luke's Parish of Beaufort District, SC:

Household # 341:

Lawton, Patience [Bing].mulatto…female….age: 53…born: SC
Lawton, Calvin L……….mulatto….male…...age: 21....born: SC
Lawton, Cathy A………..mulatto….female....age: 16…born: SC
Lawton, Margian………..mulatto….female…age: 14…born: SC
Lawton, Patience M……mulatto….female….age: 12…born: SC
Lawton, George W……..mulatto….female….age: 10…born: SC

Household # 342:

Jones, James…….mulatto…male…….age: 35……born: SC
Jones, Catherine…mulatto…female…..age: 45……born: SC
Jones, Matilda…...mulatto…female…..age: 12……born: SC
Jones, T. Ann…….mulatto…female…..age: 10…....born: SC
Jones, James M…..mulatto…male…….age: 7……..born: SC
Jones, Saint P…….mulatto…male…….age: 5……..born: SC
Jones, Richard……mulatto…male…….age: 3……..born: SC

Household # 343:

Henson, Henry……mulatto……male………age: 30……born: SC
Jones, Eugenia……mulatto……female…….age: 14……born: SC
Henson, Dedrick….mulatto……male………age: 8……..born: SC
Henson, Laura…….mulatto……female…….age: 3……..born: SC

Household # 344:

157

Bemer, Thomas......mulatto.....male.......age: 27......born: SC
Bemer, Virginia......mulatto.....female.....age: 23......born: SC
Bemer, John.........mulatto.....male........age: 2.......born: SC

Household # 355:

Williams, Betsy......mulatto......female......age: 25...born: SC
Williams, Hezekiah..mulatto......male.........age: 2......born: SC

Household # 357:

Morrison, James...mulatto......male......age: 54...born: SC
[Catawba Indian]
Morrison, Sarah....mulatto......female...age: 58...born: SC

Household # 358:

Scott, Thomas.........mulatto......male......age: 33......born: SC
Scott, Jane R..........mulatto......female....age: 27......born: SC
Scott, N................mulatto......female.....age: 6......born: SC
Scott, Kirkland........mulatto.......male.......age: 4......born: SC
Scott, Julia.............mulatto.......female.....age: 3......born: SC
Scott, Luther...........mulatto........male.......age: 1......born: SC

Household # 359:

Bing, Francis.........mulatto...male......age: 25......born: SC
Bing, Martha..........mulatto...female....age: 23......born: SC
Bing, James W........mulatto...male......age: 7.........born: SC
Bing, B. Erwin........mulatto....male......age: 6.........born: SC
Bing, Dysee E.........mulatto...female....age: 5........born: SC
Bing, Susan L.........mulatto....female....age: 4........born: SC

Household # 360:

Jones, William.........mulatto......male......age: 70......born: SC
Jenkins, Seaborne......mulatto......male.......age: 8.......born: SC

Household # 361:

Appendix 1

Jones, Cornelius......mulatto......male......age: 45.....born: SC
Jones, Jane.........mulatto......female.......age: 46.....born: SC
Jones, William E......mulatto......male......age: 20....born: SC
Jones, Albert..........mulatto.......male......age: 19...born: SC
Jones, Furman.........mulatto.......male......age: 17...born: SC
Jones, Allison..........mulatto.......male......age: 12...born: SC
Jones, Ellen............mulatto.......female.....age: 10...born: SC
Jones, Perry............mulatto.......male.......age: 4.....born: SC

Household # 362:

Jenkins, Thomas......mulatto......male......age: 35.....born: SC
Jenkins, Elsey M......mulatto......female....age: 34....born: SC
Jenkins, William C....mulatto......male......age: 14....born: SC
Jenkins, Wade H.......mulatto......male......age: 12....born: SC
Jenkins, Margaret V...mulatto......female....age: 10....born: SC
Jenkins, Horace H......mulatto......male......age: 8......born: SC
Jenkins, Josephine.....mulatto......female....age: 6.......born: SC
Jenkins, Thomas D.....mulatto......male......age: 4......born: SC
Jenkins, Cornelius R...mulatto......male......age: 1......born: SC

Household # 363:

Jones, Wesley A.........mulatto......male.......age: 36......born: SC
Jones, Mary.............mulatto.......female.....age: 26......born: SC
Jones, Dillon A..........mulatto.......male........age: 10......born: SC
Jones, Julia..............mulatto......female......age: 8........born: SC
Jones, James M..........mulatto.......male........age: 4.......born: SC
Jones, Eliza...............mulatto......female......age: 1.......born: SC
Jenkins, Minerva.........mulatto.......female......age: 11......born: SC

Household # 364:

Mims, Daniel.........mulatto.......male......age: 45......born: SC
Mims, Jane............mulatto.......female....age: 27......born: SC
Mims, James..........mulatto.......male......age: 15......born: SC
Mims, Clive............mulatto......male.......age: 12......born: SC
Mims, Nelson..........mulatto.......male......age: 10......born: SC

A Wandering Tribe

Mims, Bordary……..mulatto…….male…….age: 8……born: SC
Mims, Margaret…….mulatto…….female…..age: 6…...born: SC
Mims, Robert……….mulatto……male…….age: 4……born: SC
Mims, Jane………….mulatto……female…..age: 2……born: SC

Household # 365:

Jones, James W…..mulatto……male……….age: 36…..born: SC
Jones, Margaret…..mulatto……female…….age: 22…..born: SC

Household # 366

Radford, William Thomas…mulatto…male…age: 21…born: SC

Household # 367:

Jones, Daniel…....black…male…….age: 53…....born: SC
Jones, Rebecca....black....female…..age: 48…....born: SC
Jones, Willis…...black…male…….age: 22…....born: SC
Jones, J Wesley...black…male…….age: 20…....born: SC
Jones, M………..black…female…..age: 19…....born: SC
Jones, Morgan….black…male…….age: 17…....born: SC
Jones, Frederick...black….male…...age: 16…....born: SC
Jones, Hardy……black…male……age: 14…....born: SC
Jones, Barney…...black…male…….age: 12……born: SC
Jones, Josiah…….black…male……age: 10……born: SC
Jones, Calvin……black…male…….age: 8……..born: SC
Jones, Sally……..black….female…..age: 6……born: SC
Jones, Mary O…..black…female…...age: 4…….born: SC
Jones, Raymond…black…male…….age: 2…….born: SC

Household # 368:

Scott, Ann……mulatto…female……age: 56……born: SC
Scott, Elijah….mulatto…male……….age: 23……born: SC
Scott, Mary C...mulatto…female…….age: 10…...born: SC

Household # 369:

Appendix 1

Williams, Stephen...mulatto....male......age: 54.........born: SC
Williams, Ann.........mulatto...female....age: 52.........born: SC
Williams, Sarah A....mulatto...female....age: 15.........born: SC
Williams, Milly H....mulatto....female...age: 13.........born: SC
Williams, George.....mulatto....male......age: 12.........born: SC
Williams, Calvin......mulatto....male......age: 10.........born: SC
Williams, Parmanter..mulatto.....male......age: 3.........born: SC

Household # 370:

Jones, Francis......mulatto......male......age: 22......born: SC
Jones, Harriet.......mulatto......female....age: 19........born: SC
Jones, Eliza.........mulatto......female....age: 1........born: SC

Household # 371:

Bing, Matthew............mulatto.....male......age: 56....born: SC
Bing, Caroline [Bignold]mulatto.....female....age: 51....born: SC
Bing, Caroline E..........mulatto......female....age: 25...born: SC
Bing, Salina...............mulatto......female....age: 22....born: SC
Bing, Lisbon...............mulatto......male......age: 20...born: SC
Bing, Laura................mulatto......female....age: 18...born: SC
Bing, Mary H..............mulatto......female....age: 14...born: SC
Bing, Joel McF............mulatto......male......age: 10...born: SC
Bing, Thaddeus E.........mulatto......male......age: 8.....born: SC
Bing, Eugnenia Primus...mulatto......female...age: 14...born: SC
Bing, Elvira................mulatto......female....age: 12...born: SC
Bing, Eugene..............mulatto.......male.....age: 10...born: SC

Household # 372:

Busbee, Amos......mulatto......male........age: 55.......born: SC
Busbee, Fanny [Jones]...mulatto...female...age: 37.......born: SC
Busbee, Alice............mulatto....female...age: 11......born: SC
Busbee, Mary............mulatto....female...age: 9........born: SC
Busbee, Patrick..........mulatto.....male......age: 6.......born: SC
Busbee, Emma...........mulatto....female....age: 4.......born: SC
Busbee, Melissa..........mulatto....female....age: 2.......born: SC
Busbee, Julia.............mulatto...female....age: 1..... ..born: SC

A Wandering Tribe

Household # 373:

Ferrell, Thomas.........mulatto....male.......age: 25....born: SC
Ferrell, Sarah E.F.M. ...mulatto...female.....age: 18.....born: SC
Ferrell, Laura A.........mulatto...female.....age: 1.......born: SC

Household # 374:

Newton, Robert......mulatto......male......age: 53......born: SC
Newton, Ann..........mulatto......female....age: 50......born: SC

Household # 375:

Busbee, Jeremiah......mulatto......male......age: 50...born: SC
Busbee, Eliza...........mulatto......female....age: 54...born: SC
Busbee, Catherine......mulatto......female....age: 14...born: SC
Busbee, Keziah A......mulatto......female....age: 13...born: SC
Busbee, Rachel.........mulatto......female....age: 12...born: SC
Busbee, Lawrence......mulatto......male......age: 11...born: SC
Busbee, Jedediah........mulatto......male......age: 10...born: SC
Busbee, Edward.........mulatto......male......age: 7....born: SC
Busbee, Washington....mulatto......male.......age: 6...born: SC

Household # 376:

Jones, Ralph..........mulatto.......male......age: 41...born: SC
Jones, Sarah A.......mulatto.......female...age: 38....born: SC
Jones, Thomas E.....mulatto.......male......age: 18....born: SC
Jones, Boufort........mulatto.......male......age: 16....born: SC
Jones, Ralph..........mulatto.......male......age: 14....born: SC
Jones, Lizzy A........mulatto.......male......age: 11....born: SC
Jones, Gaskin.........mulatto........male......age: 7......born: SC

Appendix 1

BEAMER

William Beamer (born circa 1762) was a full-blooded Indian of unknown tribal origin. In 1850 he married Rachel Eady (mixed white and Catawba Indian) in a ceremony officiated by Colonel McElney.

William Beamer served in Roebuck's South Carolina Regiment in the Revolutionary War and was wounded at the Battle of Cowpens.

William Beamer	**Rachel Eady**
Born: 1762 South Carolina	born: South Carolina

Children:
- Eliza Beamer (born 6 July 1810 South Carolina)
- Rebecca "Kiziah" Beamer (born 1 Aug 1812 South Carolina)
- William Beamer (born 17 Jan 1812 South Carolina)
- John Beamer (born 25 Sept 1817 South Carolina)
- Jane Beamer (born circa 1819 South Carolina)
- Sarah Catherine Beamer (born 27 Oct 1822 South Carolina)
- Joseph Beamer (born 16 Sept 1825 South Carolina)

20 March 1821:

Affidavit of W. S. Smith Officer of Common Pleas, Charleston district:

> *"I certify that in the case of Rachel Beamer and others, stating that they were the descendants of a free Indian woman in amity with this state. An Order restrained the Tax Collector of St. Phillips and St. Michaels from levying and collecting any tax has been granted by the Honorable Judge Bay."*

20 Aug 1821:

Affidavit of P. N. Lindenboom:

> *"...that Diana Beamer is the daughter of a free Indian woman named Rachel Beamer and that she hath two children, one*

named Kitty (a girl aged 5 years and one month) and the other named George (a boy about one year and four months)."

5 Feb 1822:

Affidavit of John Hinckley Mitchell, Notary Public, City of Charleston:

...appeared before me...Rachel Beamer of Johns Island, of a dark complexion but the descendant of a free Indian woman...says that one black boy about the age of 12 years, named William Beamer; another boy, a mulatto, about the age of 3 years, named Thomas Albert Dunmeyer, and one girl child, a mulatto about the age of 7 years, named Elizabeth Dunmeyer are all them bona fide the children and issue of this deponent, the said Rachel Beamer. And are all now living on Johns Island.

21 June 1847:
Affidavit of Hugh Wilson of the parish of St. Johns, Colleton County, SC:

...I am well acquainted with William Beamer, an American Indian aged about 85 years. I have known him upwards of 25 years, during the greater part of which time he has had residence on Johns Island...the citizens of said Island have always treated him as an Indian...I believe him to be of Indian descent."

21June 1847:
Affidavit of William Beamer, St. Johns Island, Colleton County, SC:

...I have always considered myself as of Indian descent...Jane Beamer, Eliza Beamer and Rebecca Beamer now before the court I believe to be my children. Besides these three daughters, I have three sons: John, Joseph and William. I was duly married to their mother, Rachel Eady, by Col. McElney. Said children were born in lawful wedlock. I believe my wife to be

Appendix 1

> *Indian when I married her. Such status has never been denied her."*

17 Jan 1851:
Affidavit of Robert Anderson:

> *...he had known John Beamer, William Beamer, Joseph Beamer, Eliza Beamer, Keziah Beamer, and Jane Beamer for 18 years...they have always been regarded as the children of William Beamer and Rachel Beamer. William Beamer was considered a full-blooded Indian. Rachel Beamer was mixed white and Indian."*

Mary Beamer (born circa 1740) was full-blooded Indian of unknown tribal origin. She lived in St. John's Parish, Colleton County, SC.

16 Aug 1802:
Affidavit of Joseph Stanyarne, St. John'sParish, Colleton County, SC:

> *...sayeth I knew an Indian woman named Mary Beamer, which resided on the plantation of Mr. John Stanyarne....she was a free woman...her daughter, also named Mary Beamer, was likewise free. And she had two sons the oldest of which was called William and the other Sam or Samuel. The last two mentioned persons are now alive, the eldest of whom is about 40 years of age, and the other about 36."*

10 Feb 1824:
Affidavit of Benjamin Reynolds of St. Johns Island, Colleton County, SC:

> *...I hereby certify that the bearer George Eady is of the family of Mary Beamer, and that the said Mary descended from one of the tribe of Indians in amity with the white."*

A Wandering Tribe

BING

Eliza Bing (born circa 1790 St. Luke's, SC) was a full-blooded Indian of unknown tribal origin. She had children with at least three differing surnames, Bing, Brunson, and Lightwood.

10 Feb 1827:

Affidavit of Betsy (Busby) Stuart of St. James, SC:

> ...Betsy Stuart, formerly Busby, maketh oath that Eliza Bing is the descendant of an Indian. This deponent personally recollects the grandmother and the mother of said Eliza Bing...she was intimately acquainted with them and knew they were Indians...This deponent further saith that she was present when the said Eliza Bing was born. The said Eliza Bing was born of an Indian woman.

9 Mar 1827:

Affidavit of Eliza Bing of City of Charleston, SC:

> ...Eliza Bing, the descendant of an Indian mother, identifies her children as Elizabeth Lightwood age 11, Maria Lightwood age 6, Caroline Brunson age 10 months – all born in the City of Charleston.

20 Apr 1848:

Affidavit of Dr. Edward Elfe of the City of Charleston, SC:

> ...made oath that he knows Emmeline Cooper, a free brown girl now in the 17th year of her age. She is the daughter of Elizabeth Lightwood named in the foregoing affidavit...she had the reputation of being descended from Indian Pedigree in the maternal line.

Appendix 1

21 Feb 1860:

Affidavit of J. Dickson Bruns M.D. of the City of Charleston, SC:

> ...*do testify that Moses Bing (alias Brunson) aged about 9 years and John Bing (alias Brunson) aged about 4 years are the children of Caroline Bing (alias Brunson), whose free Indian papers are duly recorded in the Secretary of State's Office, Charleston, South Carolina in Miscellaneous Records Book 5C, page 498.*

17 May 1861:

Affidavit of Reverend J. Claudius Miller, City of Charleston, SC:

> ...*swears that he is well acquainted with Maria Bing, now Bates. That she was employed in his family as a general servant for a length of time and that she bore a most excellent character...the said Maria has two children now living, to wit Eliza Bates aged 15 years and Henry Bates aged 10 years...the said Maria is the descendant of a free Indian woman.*

A Wandering Tribe

Laura Bing
1807-1868

Appendix 1

Julius Bing
1836-1893

A Wandering Tribe

BOZZARD

18 Aug 1823:

Affidavit of Betsy Busby of St. Luke's, SC:
"Betsy Busby deposeth that William Bozzard about 21 years of age, Jane Bozzard about 15 years of age, Mosley Bozzard about 12 years of age, Eliza Bozzard about 8 years of age and Nancy Bozzard about 26 years of age are her children."

BUSBY

Thomas Busby (born 1674 unknown) who was an "Indyan boy" servant of Robert Caufield of Surry County Virginia.

Betsy Busby (born circa 1780 South Carolina) a full-blooded Indian of unknown tribal origin. She had children with at least six differing surnames, Bing, Bozzard, Brunson, Saints, Scott, and Stuart.

1 Feb 1810:

Affidavit of Betsy Busby of St. Luke's, SC:

> *...Betsy Busby, being Indian born, the first child born, Nancy Busby likewise, the said Nancy being born an Indian – were exempted from taxes. Therefore, all the children are the same. Hear follows the Children: Lizar Bing [Eliza Bing Gordon], Abraham Scott, Mary Scott, John Bruton, Martha Scott. Witnesses: William Gordon, Edward Saints.*

3 Nov 1819:

Affidavit of Lewis Roux of St. Luke's, SC:

Appendix 1

...Personally appeared Betsy Busby (formerly Betsy Saints) who made oath that Edward Saints living at Middle Plantation on Ashely River is her son by David Saints, an Englishman.

3 Nov 1819:

Affidavit of Elizabeth Peake of St. Luke's, SC:
>...*deposeth that she was well acquainted with the grandmother, mother and father of the within named Betsy Busby, that they were Indians.*

18 Aug 1823:

Affidavit of Betsy Busby of St. Luke's, SC:

>...Betsy Busby deposeth that William Bozzard about 21 years of age, Jane Bozzard about 15 years of age, Molsey Bozzard about 12 years of age, Eliza Bozzard about 8 years of age and Nancy Bozzard about 26 years of age are her children.

A Wandering Tribe

Margie Ann Busby
1883-1945

Appendix 1

Henry Busby
Son of Isham Busby and Mary Bing
B: 1823 St. Luke's Parish, Beaufort Co. SC
D: 1875 Eucheanna, Walton Co. FL

A Wandering Tribe

FERRELL

15 Oct 1849:
Affidavit of Miss Ann Duval of Colleton District, SC:

> *...She well knew one George Ferrell to have resided in said district [Colleton] during the time she lived there...he was always taken for a Free Indian. He had a sister named Francis who intermarried with one Parker, who died. She afterwards married one James Johnson who was a white man. Francis was a free Indian.*

12 Nov 1849:
Affidavit of John Edwards of Colleton District, SC:

> *...Francis Ferrell intermarried with one Parker likewise a free Indian. The said Francis Parker otherwise Francis Johnson and the said James Johnson have long since died.*

HENSON

Sarah Henson (born circa 1780 Beaufort District Indian Settlement) was at least ½ Indian of unknown tribal origin.

21 May 1818:
Affidavit of Mary Smith of the St. Luke's, Beaufort SC:
"...declared that she well knew Sarah Hamlin who was a free Indian woman. And that she was the mother of Sarah Hinson, now living in Charleston. And that Catherine Jordan, Susannah Hinson, and Elizabeth Hinson are the daughters of the above said Sarah Hinson."

Mary Henson (born circa 1780 St. Luke's Indian Settlement) was at least ½ Indian of unknown tribal origin.
13 March 1824:
Certificate issued by Joseph Bennett, City Treasurer, Charleston, SC:

Appendix 1

"I do hereby certify that Mary M. Hinson is of Indian descent."

15 October 1825:
Court case of State of South Carolina V. Mary Hinson:
"I do hereby certify that Mary Hinson was brought up before me…charged with having returned into the State contrary to Law and that the following is the verdict of the said Court, "We find the Defendant not ameniable to the Act of 1823 [law forbidding Free Negroes to enter the State], she being of free Indian Descent."

JACKSON

11 Feb 1824:
Affidavit of unnamed individual recorded in City of Charleston, SC:
"…Rebecca Jackson descends from a free Indian woman."

19 Dec 1825:
Affidavit of Thomas Scott of the City of Charleston:
"…swears that Henry Jackson, about 19 years of age, is the son of Rebecca Jackson who is the daughter of a free Indian woman."

JONES

1755:
South Carolina Commissions of Indians:
"Lewis Jones, headman of the Pee Dee Indians."

21 June 1783:
Pay Bill for Capt Thomas Drennan's Company of Catawba Indians under the Command of Gen Sumter":
Enlisted: Jammy Jones

9 Dec 1859:
Petition to the Honorable Legislature of South Carolina, originating from Edgefield District, SC:

"Petition of Frederick Chavis, Lewis Chavis, Durany Chavis, James Jones, Bartley Jones, Mary Jones, Jonathan Williams, and Polly Dunn…the first six petitioners above named, to wit, the Chavis and Jones families, are free persons of color being descendants of Indian ancestors. Pray your Honorable body to say whether by free persons of color, they mean to include descendants of Indians, or only those who are mixed with negro blood."

MIMS

14 June 1894:
The News and Courier article:
"A Leading Citizen of Hampton Waylaid and Shot Dead – A Mestizo Arrested on Suspicion – Hampton June 13- Capt. James Mixson of the 'Steep Bottom' neighborhood of this county, was waylaid and shot to death Monday, the 11th, while returning home at night from his place of business. Candry Mims has been arrested under suspicion of being the assassin. Mims, who is suspected of having done the deed, is one of a rather peculiar race of people who live in the river section of the county, locally known as 'Old Issue'. They are a mixed race, and have never been slaves. They are supposed to be descendants of Indians, but nothing is definitely known of their origin."

WILLIAMS

21 June 1783:
Pay Bill for Capt Thomas Drennan's Company of Catawba Indians under the command of Gen Sumpter:
Served: Billey Williams

24 Nov 1792:
Petition of the Chief and Head Men of the Catawba Nation:
Signed: Billey Williams

Appendix 1

9 July 1802:
Affidavit of William Bleehendon of Prince William's Parish, Beafort District, SC:

> "...affirmeth that Bathsheba the wife of Reuben Ironmonger, is either an Half Breed or an Indian and is and was always deemed an Indian descendant and never reckoned as Mestizoe or Mulattoe."

16 June 1823:
Affidavit of Mary Avinger of Orangeburg District, SC:

> "...she has always inferred and verily believes that Hanah Williams and Bashaba Ironmonger was own sisters by their mother's side, and Lydia Ivey, Lewis Williams and Leven Victor Williams were brothers and sister, and that they were children of the said Hanah Williams."

21 Nov 1823:
Affidavit of William Allan, Elizabeth Bounetheau, Elizabeth Nacyl, William Read, and Sarah Russell of the City of Charleston:

> "We do hereby certify that we are well acquainted with and knew John Williams and Mary or Molly Williams, his wife...were well known by every other person to be both of them born from Cherokee Indians...And who died on about the 20th of August, 1804."

9 Dec 1859:
Petition to the Honorable Legislature of South Carolina, originating from Edgefield District, SC:

> "Petition of Frederick Chavis, Lewis Chavis, Durany Chavis, James Jones, Bartley Jones, Mary Jones, Jonathan Williams, and Polly Dunn...the first six petitioners above named, to wit, the Chavis and Jones families, are free persons of color being descendants of Indian ancestors. Pray your Honorable body to say whether by free persons of color, they mean to include descendants of Indians, or only those who are mixed with Negro blood."

A Wandering Tribe

Appendix 2

WESTERN CATAWBA INDIAN ASSOCIATION

James A Bain was President of the Catawba Indian Association.

George E Williamson was Secretary of the Catawba Indian Association.

1 March 1888:
Article appearing in Indian Chieftain Newspaper, Vinita, Indian Territory:

> *"The Western Catawba Indian Association, with headquarters in Fort Smith, proposes to petition congress to set aside for the use of all persons of Indian blood, not members of any tribe, a portion of the Indian Territory."*

16 August 1889:
Article "Catawba Indian Association" within The Fort Smith Elevator newspaper, Fort Smith, ARK:

> *"The Catawba Indian Association met at Rocky Ridge on the 10th. The meeting was called to order by the President. After the reading of the minutes and the calling of the roll of the officers, transacting other business that came before the order, a call for new members was made and 90 was added to the new list, after which the meeting adjourned to meet at Aults' Mill, three miles south of Fort Smith, the second day of the fair, the 16th day of October, where the delegates and all persons interested will please attend without further notice, as matters of interest will be considered. J. Bain, President, G. W. Williamson, Secretary"*

October 16, 1889:

A Wandering Tribe

Article "Attention Catawbas" within The Fort Smith Elevator newspaper:

> "The Western Catawbas Indian Association met at Ault's Mill October 16, 1889, at which meeting a number of new members were added to the Association, thus making it nearly 4,000 strong. They appointed an executive committee which is empowered to transact all business and place the matter before congress. The Association adjourned to convene again at a called meeting of the president."

Jan 1895:
Article appearing within The Fort Smith Elevator newspaper:

> "All Catawba Indians by blood or otherwise are requested to meet at the County Court House in Fort Smith Arkansas on Thursday, Jan 24th, 1895 at 10 o'clock a. m. for the purpose of perfecting the census roll of the Western Catawba Indian Association and the transaction of other matters that may come before the meeting. All Catawba Indians are expected to be present or by proxy as business of importance will come before the meeting. James Bain, Pres't. Geo. E. Williams, Sec'ry."

1972:

> .....The Last Trek of the Indians" by Grant Foreman, Chapter XIX, Small Tribes, Page 319:
> By reason of their dispersed condition, and their neglect by the federal government, the Catawba in the west did not benefit by the co-called "Allotment Act of 1887" and became scattered in and about the future Oklahoma, living in the manner of the White People, whose blood many of them possessed. In an effort to improve their condition, a convention of the Catawba was held in Fort Smith, Arkansas, on April 25, 1895, where efforts were made to organize and present to Congress their claims to allotments of lands. This convention was composed of representatives of 257 persons of Catawba

Appendix 2

blood living in the Creek and Choctaw nations and throughout Western Arkansas. Of those in attendance, 125 were from Arkansas. Greenwood in that state was the home of 44, the largest from any town; of the 132 living in Indian Territory, 17 claimed Checotah as their post office; and Starr was the home of 34. Perhaps most conspicuous of these Catawba was "Judge" Leblanche, who was among the Catawba Indians admitted into the Creek Tribe and who became a prominent merchant and cattleman living near Checota, Indian territory. The Indians who assembled at Fort Smith set up a permanent organization, elected officers, and planned subordinate Catawba Associations in respective localities of members. The main convention adopted a preamble, resolutions, and bylaws. Under the name of the "Catawba and Non-reservation Indians Convention," with James Bain as chairman and George E. Williamson as secretary, the proceedings were incorporated in a memorial which was forwarded to Congress, whence in turn it was referred to the Secretary of the Interior for investigation and report. The Commissioner of Indian Affairs thereupon prepared the desired report, which the Senate, on September 23, 1897, ordered to be printed, and which became Senate Document 144 (54th Cong, 2d sess.) This report is exhaustive and contains all the history of these Indians within the knowledge of the Office of Indian Affairs at that time.

February 23rd, 1897:
"The Catawba Tribe of Indians" Senate Report 54th Congress, Second Session, Document #144:

> ....Sir, I am in receipt, by department reference, of ???? a memorial in behalf of the individuals formerly comprising and belonging to the Catawba tribe of Indians, with request that the inquiries contained in said memorial be answered and information concerning the statements therein and the appended memorandum be furnished. The memorial submitted by Senator Pettigrew is signed by James Bain, President, and George

A Wandering Tribe

E. Williamson, secretary, of the Catawba Indian Association, and they ask on behalf of the individuals formerly comprising and belonging to the Catawba Tribe of Indians, to be informed "as to the status of the tribal lands of the Catawba Indians formerly belonging to the Catawba Tribe of Indians, and to secure anything that might be due them as accruing from said lands; and also to receive any or further relief, help or benefits they may be found, upon careful investigation of the facts in their case, to be entitled to receive in right, justice, or equity from the United States or otherwise in the matter of new homes in the west or to their lands in the east.

D. M. Browning, commissioner

Petition to the Secretary of the Interior:

To the Senate and House of Representatives of the United States of America in Congress Assembled,

>......Your petitioners come representing that they are representatives of the individuals and their descendants who were formerly the members of the Catawba Tribe of Indians that owned and occupied lands in the states of North Carolina and South Carolina, that in pursuance of the policy of the United States to remove all the Indian tribes to new homes to be provided for them west of the Mississippi River, Congress passed an act July 19, 1848, appropriating $5,000 for the removal of the Catawba Tribe, with their own consent, to the west of the Mississippi River, and for settling them and subsisting them one year in new homes first to be obtained for them (9 Stat L. 164); that nothing was accomplished under this act; that the provisions and appropriations thereof were reenacted in the act of July 31, 1854 (10 Stat. L. , 316); that some efforts were made to secure for the Catawbas new homes among the Choctaw and Chickasaw Indians of the Indian Territory . . . The present location and number of those Catawba Indians who went west, expecting to be located on lands west of the Mississippi River by the Department of the Interior are as follows,

Appendix 2

as furnished by James Bain, President of the Catawba Indian Association at Fort Smith, Ark.:

Greenwood, Ark., 44; Barber, Ark., 42; Crow, Ark., 13; Oak Bower, Ark., 3; Enterprise, Ark., 6; Fort Smith, Ark., 17. Total Arkansas, 125.

Checotah, Ind. T., 17; Texanna, Ind. T., 15; Jackson, Ind. T., 15; Star, Ind. T., 34; Panther, Ind. T., 22; Oaklodge, Ind. T., 10; Redland, Ind. T., 4; Rainville, Ind. T., 2; Indianola, Ind. T., 3; Center, Ind. T., 4; Ward, Ind. T., 3; Sacred Heart, Ind. T., 1; Steigler, Ind. T., 2. Total 132.

Grand Total 257."

March 28, 1896:

Letter of Department of the Interior, Office of Indian Affairs, Washington, DC:

> ...Sir, I am in receipt of your letter of Feb 22 . . .in the matter of the claims and demands of the Catawba Indian Association to the United States, published at Fort Smith, Arkansas, giving the proceedings of a convention of Catawba Indians held in that city April 15, 1895, called for the purpose of considering the condition, status and welfare of all Catawba and non-reservation Indians, and to take action in proclaiming an allotment of land under the fourth section of the general allotment act of Feb. 8, 1887 (24 Stat. L., p. 388) as amended by the act of Feb., 28, 1891 (26 Stat. L. p. 795.). This memorial purports to come from the Catawba Indians, comprising they allege, "all persons of Catawba descent, and their descendants, including all persons who have intermarried with Catawba Indians, and all persons of mixed Catawba and White blood and descent residing in any of the states and territories of the United States or in Indian Territory", claiming further that the United States has never made any provisions for them. You suggest that arrangements might be made whereby they

A Wandering Tribe

could take land in severalty within the Kiowa, Comanche and Wichita reservations, Oklahoma Territory, when the unallotted lands of said reservations shall be opened to settlement. In reply I have to reply that the Catawba Indians are a division of North American Indians which included in the last century about 28 confederated tribes. The few survivors of this people are on the Catawba Reservation in York County, South Carolina. There have been frequent communications from and concerning the Catawba Indians since 1888, but none involving or furnishing any new facts of information concerning the history or status of these Indians or their lands. I know of no reason why these Individual Indians may not take up lands in severalty under the fourth section of the act of 1887 aforesaid. I do not think it would be practicable or wise to ask the President to withhold from public settlement the land ceded by the Kiowa and Comanche Indians by their last agreement, when that agreement is ratified by Congress, until such Indians had first taken allotments thereon. They could conform to the act of 1887 as all other Indians in like condition have to do. The memorial is herewith returned, Very respectfully, D. M. Browning, commissioner.

1860 census of Illinois District, Pope County, Arkansas:

Household # 100:

Williamson, Harriet……...white…....female….age: 49.....born: Tenn
Williamson, Sarah L……..white…....female….age: 23.....born: ARK
Williamson, Robert F…....white…....male……age: 20.....born: ARK
Williamson, George M.....white…....male……age: 13....born: ARK
Williamson, Joseph……....white…....male…….age: 10....born: ARK

1870 Census of Dover, Pope County, Arkansas:

Household # 179:

Appendix 2

Williamson, George M…white……male…..age: 23….born: ARK
Williamson, Nancy R…..white……female...age: 21….born: ARK
Williamson, Sarah Ann....white…...female…age: 1…..born: ARK

1870 census of Carter, Ashley County, Arkansas:

Household # 131:

Bain, Samuel……white……..male……..age: 55……born: SC
Bain, Nancie…….white……..female…...age: 34……born: Ala
Bain, John……….white……..male……..age: 18……born: Ala
Bain, James……...white……..male……..age: 16……born: Miss
Bain, George…….white……..male……..age: 10……born: Miss
Bain, William……white……..male……..age: 7……..born: Miss
Bain, Dolphis…….white……..male……..age: 4……..born: Miss
Bain, Emma………white…….female…...age: 1……..born: Miss

1880 census of Eleven point, Randolph County, Arkansas:

Household # 156:

Williamson, John……white…...male…..age: 65….born: Missouri
Williamson, Eliza…...white…..female....age: 40…..born: Tenn
Williamson, George....white…...male…..age: 15…..born: Missouri
Williamson, Ellar……white….female….age: 14…..born: Missouri
Williamson, Julia…….white….female….age: 12…..born: Missouri
Williamson, Nancy…..white….female….age: 9…...born: Missouri
Williamson, John…….white…..male……age: 5…...born: Missouri

1900 census of Lewis, Scott County, Arkansas:

Household # 148:

Williamson, George.....white…male……age: 35…..born: Missouri
Williamson, Nancy J....white...female…..age: 29…..born: Ark
Williamson, Pairglee…white...female…..age: 10…..born: Ark

Williamson, Lauren…..white…female….age: 7……born: Ark
Williamson, Leon…….white…male……age: 5……born: Ark
Williamson, Loyed……white…male……age: 1….....born: Ark

1900 census of Illinois District, Pope County, Arkansas:

Household # 49:

Williamson, George M..white…male……age: 53….born: ARK
Williamson, Mary……..white…female….age: 36….born: Illinois
Williamson, Kellie J…..white…female....age: 26….born: ARK
Williamson, Ruby……..white…female....age: 20….born: ARK
Williamson, Boyd……..white….male…...age: 17…born: ARK
Williamson, Bertha……white…female.....age: 6…..born: ARK
Williamson, Dollie….white……female….age: 4…..born: ARK
Williamson, Joe……..white…….male……age: 1…..born: ARK

1910 census of Heavener, LeFlore County, Oklahoma:

Household # 205:

Williamson, George E…white…male……age: 44….born: Missouri
Williamson, Nancy…….white…female…age: 39….born: Ark
Williamson, Parylee……white…female…age: 20….born: Ark
Williamson, Laura……...white…female…age: 17….born: Ark
Williamson, Leon……….white….male…...age: 15…born: Ark
Williamson, Selma……..white….female….age: 3…..born: OK

1910 census of Pine Bluff, Jefferson County, Arkansas:

Household # 55:

Bain, James A……..white……..male……….age: 52……born: ARK
Bain, Anna E……….white……..female…….age: 29……born: ARK
Bain, Jimmerta A…..white……..female…….age: 9……..born: ARK
Bain, James A Jr……white……..male……….age: 7……..born: ARK

Appendix 2

Bain, Marion A……..white…….female…….age: 5…..…born: ARK

1920 census of Sugarloaf, Sebastian County, Arkansas:
Household # 103:

Bain, James………..white……..male……….age: 71……born: Miss
Bain, Orral………....white……..female…….age:28……born: ARK

1920 census of Red Fork, Tulsa County, Oklahoma:
Household # 42:

Bain, Bradley………white……..male……….age: 26……born: Tenn
Bain, Clydia………..white……..female……..age: 25……born: Geo
Bain, Paul G………..white……..male……….age: 3…..…born: Tex
Bain, Dallas………...white……..male……….age: 2…..…born: Ok
Bain, Howard……….white……..male……….age: 1…..…born: Ok
Bain, James M…..…white……..male……….age: 65……born: Tenn

1920 census of Cordell, Washita County, Oklahoma:
Household # 175:

Williamson, George……white…..male……age: 37…..born: Tenn
Williamson, Bell M……white…...female….age: 30…..born: Tex
Williamson, Irine T…….white…..female…age: 15……born: Ok
Williamson, Freda L……white…..female…age: 6…….born: OK
Williamson, Mildred…...white…..female….age: 4…….born: Ok
Williamson, G W……….white…..male……age: 2……born: Ok

1930 census of Bayliss, Pope County, Arkansas:
Household # 52:

Williamson, Boyd……white…male…..age: 48….born: ARK

A Wandering Tribe

Williamson, Rena......white...female...age: 42.....born: ARK
Williamson, Jewel......white...female...age: 21....born: ARK
Williamson, Gewell....white...male......age: 17...born: ARK
Williamson, Bessie M...white...female...age: 16...born: ARK
Williamson, Chester M..white...male.....age: 12....born: ARK
Williamson, Noma L.....white...female...age: 8....born: ARK
Williamson, B W.........white...male.....age: 4.....born: ARK
Williamson, George W....white...male....age: 83...born: ARK

1930 census of Anson, Jones County, Texas:

Household # 180:

Williamson, George.....white.....male.....age: 48......born: Tenn
Williamson, Bell.........white....female...age: 38......born: Tex
Williamson, Freda........white....female...age: 16......born: Ok
Williamson, Mildred.....white....female....age: 14.....born: Ok
Williamson, G W..........white...male......age: 12.....born: Ok
Williamson, Don.........white......male......age: 4......born: Tex
Williamson, Mary J......white.....female....age: 2......born: Tex

Appendix 3

PRE-1850 CATAWBA RECORDS

Revolutionary War Paylist of 1780:

"Pay bill for Capt Thomas Drennans Company of Catawba Indians under the command of General Thomas Sumpter in the State of South Carolina Servis- for the year 1780 and discharge in the year 1781."

1. Genr New River
2. John Brown
3. Robbin
4. Willis – deceased killed at Rock Mountain his wife & child alive
5. Suggar Jamey
6. Pinetree George
7. Morrison
8. Henry White
9. John Cagg [Kegg]
10. Quash
11. Little Mick
12. Patrick Readhead [Head]
13. Billey Williams
14. Big Jamey
15. Billey Cagg [Kegg]
16. John Connar
17. Doctor John
18. Chunkey Pipe
19. Capt Peter
20. Billey Otter
21. Little Aleck
22. John Eayrs [Ayers]
23 Petter Harris
24. Jacob Eayrs [Ayers]
25. Billey Readhead [Head]
26. John Tompson

27. Joue
28. Pattrick Brown
29. George Cantey
30. Jacob Scott
31. Bobb
32. James Eayrs [Ayers]
33. Little Stephen
34. Little Charley
35. John Celliah [Kennedy]
36. Petter George
37. George White
38. Jack Simmons
39. Billey Scott
40. Young John
41. Tom Cook

White Men: Mathew Brown, Michael Delou, Ralph Smith

"Attached list of those Indians who did service which cannot be vouched for, 1780-1781:"

1. John Morrison
2. Captain Quash
3. Colonel John Eayrs [Ayers]
4. John Kelliah [Kennedy]
5. Jammy Jones
6. Gilber [Gilbert George]
7. Capt Redhead [Head]
8. Tom Cross
9. George Harris
10. Chickesaw Jimmy
11. John Nettles

Petition of "the Chief and Head Men of Cataba Nation" 24 November 1792:

1. General New River
2. Colonel John Ears [Ayers]
3. Major John Brown
4. Captain Peter

Appendix 3

5. Captain Jacob Scott
6. Captain Thomas Cook
7. Captain Jammy
8. Captain John Scott
9. Captain John Cagg [Kegg]
10. Jammy Bullen
11. Jammy Ears [Ayers]
12. Peter George
13. George White
14. Pinetree George
15. Billey Williams
16. Jacob Ears [Ayers]
17. Billey Scott
18. John Kennedy
19. Patrick Dickson
20. Pinetree Robbin
21. Tom Patterson
22. John Nettles
23. George Canty
24. John Yong
25. Billy Readhead [Head]
26. John Ears [Ayers]
27. John Kelley
28. John Deloe [1/2 breed son of Michael Delou]
29. Billy Ears [Ayers]
30. Gilbert George
31. Chickeshaw Jammy

Catawba Census of 1849:

In 1849 South Carolina Governor Seabrook ordered B.S. Massey, the Indian Agent assigned oversight of the Catawba Indians, to perform a census of all Catawba Indians still connected to their old reservation homes, or those living among the Cherokee in western North Carolina. Massey provided the following list:

A Wandering Tribe

A List of Names of Catawba Indians, residing in North Carolina, Haywood County, Cherokee Nation:

1. James Kegg................age: 66
2. Phillip Kegg................age: 22
3. Billey George................age: 33
4. Lewis Stephens............age: 46
5. Thomas Stephens..........age: 18
6. Antoney George............age: 50
7. Jessey Harris................age: 17
8. William Morrison.........age: 33
9. John Hart....................age: 30
10. Peter Harris...............age: 14
11. James Harris..............age: 16
12. John Harris................age: 18
(12 male children under the age of ten)
13. Nancey George...........age: 44
14. Rebeccah George........age: 36
15. Harriot Stephens.........age: 44
16. Margaret Ayers...........age: 18
17. Betsey Ayers..............age: 19
18. Salley Harris..............age: 43
19. Frankey Brown...........age: 27
20. Julia Ann Ayers...........age: 15
21. Susy Kegg..................age: 21
22. Cyntha Kegg...............age: 30
23. Mary Ayers.................age: 21
24. Mary Ayers.................age: 12
25. Salley Readhead [Head]age: 60
26. Polly Stephens..............age: 24
27. Sally Ayers...................age: 50
28. Salley George...............age: 35
(15 female children under the age of ten)

A List of Names of Catawba Indians, residing in South Carolina, Chester District:
1. Allen Harris....................age: 35
2. Sam Scott......................age: 50

Appendix 3

3. Robert Mush……………….age: 19
(3 male children under the age of ten)
4. Rody Harris………………..age: 19
5. Jiney Patterson……………..age: 30
6. Martha Patterson……………age: 18
7. Nancey George……………..age: 70
8. Little Nancy George………..age: 24
(2 female children under the age of ten)

A List of Names of Catawba Indians, residing in South Carolina, Greenville District:

1. Franklin Canty……………..age: 23
2. John Brown…………………age: 12
3. Billey Brown……………….age: 20
4. John Scott…………………..age: 23
5. David Harris………………..age: 40
(2 male children under the age of ten)
6. Polley Ayers………………..age: 35
7. Eliza Canty…………………age: 23
8. Caty Joe……………………age: 50
9. Jane Ayers………………….age: 18
10. Jinny Joe………………….age: 43
11. Mary George……………...age: 18
12. Patsey George…………….age: 48
13. Betsey Mush……………...age: 18
14. Patsey George…………….age: 30
15. Rachel Brown……………..age: 35
16. Esther Brown……………..age: 28
17. Polly Readhead [Head]……..age: 40
18. Betsey Hart……………….age: 26
19. Peggey Canty……………..age: 20
(6 female children under the age of ten)

A List of Names of Catawba Indians, residing in South Carolina, York District:

1. Betsey Quash………………age: 60
2. Susey Quash……………….age: 35

A Wandering Tribe

3. Delphy Quash……………………...age: 32
4. Nancey Quash……………………..age: 37
5. Peggy Quash……………………….age: 25
6. Rachel Quash…………………….age: 30
7. Polley Ayers……………………..age: 35
(3 male children under the age of ten)
(4 female children under the age of ten)

INDEX

A

Alexander, 62, 67, 73, 137, 138, 142, 144, 147, 148, 149, 157
Alexander Goings. *See*
Appalachee, 19, 57
Ayers, 101, 196, 197, 198, 199, 200, 201

B

Bain, 186, 187, 188, 190, 192, 193, 194
Bates, 175
Beale, x, 109
Beamer, 37, 171, 172, 173
Bennett, 40, 181
Bing, x, 4, 63, 117, 118, 125, 157, 158, 160, 161, 163, 165, 166, 169, 173, 174, 175, 176, 177, 180
Bluit, 38
Bozzard, 177, 178
Breech, 15, 16, 19, 21, 37
Brown, x, 7, 15, 16, 17, 18, 19, 20, 37, 57, 63, 64, 102, 103, 157, 196, 197, 198, 199, 200
Brunson, 125, 173, 174, 177
Buck, 77
Bunch, 19, 20, 21
Burbage, 59
Burckmeyer, 96
Busby, x, 4, 63, 125, 157, 158, 159, 163, 173, 174, 177, 178, 179, 180

C

Cagg, 7, 97, 196, 198
Calhoun County, Florida, 126, 127, 137
Canty, x, 23, 24, 25, 41, 102, 147, 150, 198, 200, 201
Celliah, 7, 197
Chavers, x, 65, 102, 103, 104, 107, 108, 109, 111, 125, 139, 140, 143
Chavis, 59, 105, 107, 183, 185
Cheraw, 1, 3, 6, 7, 77
Cherokee, xi, 2, 9, 10, 11, 13, 14, 29, 42, 43, 44, 65, 66, 69, 81, 97, 98, 99, 117, 121, 123, 131, 132, 133, 184, 199
Choctaw, 11, 66, 77, 82, 98, 117, 123, 188, 189
Clark, x, 27, 28, 66, 73, 75
Coachman, 4
Cobb, 153
Cole, 28, 29, 30, 31, 32, 33, 34, 35, 36, 125
Collins, 29
Cook, 7, 197, 198
Cooke County, Texas, 2, 78, 79
Cooper, 174

195

D

Dakota Sioux, 3
Daniel Alexander, 62
Drennan, 7, 182, 183
Dunmeyer, 172
Dunn, 183, 185

E

Eady, x, 4, 15, 19, 37, 38, 40, 59, 116, 171, 172, 173
Eadytown, 37
Eayrs, 7, 196, 197
Edwards, 38, 39, 95, 181
Egyptians, 20
Ellis, 27, 148
Evans, x, 3, 41, 42, 43, 44, 45, 46, 47, 48, 49, 50, 77, 83, 84, 106, 131, 147, 150, 153, 154, 157

F

Ferrell, 95, 170, 181
Flowers, 51
Furman, x, 57, 59, 60, 116, 167

G

Gentry, x, 53, 54, 55, 112
George, 5, 7, 8, 15, 19, 30, 32, 37, 38, 63, 66, 67, 68, 72, 73, 74, 75, 76, 77, 79, 81, 86, 95, 103, 115, 119, 123, 133, 134, 135, 136, 137, 152, 158, 161, 165, 169, 171, 173, 181, 186, 188, 191, 192, 193, 194, 195, 196, 197, 198, 199, 200
Gibbs, x, 19, 57, 58, 59, 60, 157
Gibson, 35, 70, 75, 76, 94
Gill, 27
Going, 59
Goins, x, 57, 58, 59, 60, 61, 116
Gordon, 63, 64, 96, 125, 157, 163, 164, 177
Guy, x, 6, 65, 66, 67, 68, 70, 71, 72, 73, 74, 75, 76, 93, 152

H

Hagler, 101, 121
Hamlin, 181
Harris, x, 3, 7, 23, 46, 63, 77, 78, 79, 80, 102, 123, 124, 137, 148, 164, 196, 197, 199, 200
Hart, 81, 82, 133, 134, 135, 199, 201
Head, ix, x, 41, 83, 84, 85, 86, 87, 88, 89, 97, 121, 122, 123, 147, 153, 184, 196, 197, 198, 199, 201
Henagan, 9, 12
Henson, 159, 162, 165, 181
Hicks, 151
Hill, iii, v, 79, 119, 126, 127, 128, 129, 148
Hinson, 181, 182
Hosford, 103

Index

I

Indian Territory, 2, 10, 11, 43, 44, 53, 54, 66, 68, 77, 81, 82, 93, 97, 98, 111, 112, 113, 117, 123, 131, 136, 186, 188, 189, 190
Ironmonger, 184
Ivey, 184

J

Jackson, 57, 102, 134, 137, 164, 182, 190
Jacobs, 59, 116
Jeffries, x, 6, 65, 66, 91, 92, 93, 94
Joe, 21, 23, 126, 127, 193, 200
Johnson, 29, 67, 70, 76, 95, 96, 181
Jones, ix, 75, 94, 126, 157, 158, 159, 160, 161, 162, 163, 164, 165, 166, 167, 168, 169, 170, 182, 183, 185, 195, 197
Jordan, 181

K

Kegg, 9, 10, 11, 12, 97, 98, 99, 100, 121, 196, 198, 199
Kennedy, x, 101, 102, 103, 104, 105, 106, 107, 108, 109, 110, 122, 197, 198

L

Lewis, ix, 11, 38, 63, 64, 178, 182, 183, 184, 185, 192, 199
Lightwood, 173, 174
Logan, 115
Lucas, x, 59, 115, 116

M

Macon County, North Carolina, 2, 75
Marsh, 19, 119
Massey, 10, 11, 117, 138, 199
McDowell, 65, 66, 68, 93
McGhee, 109
McIntosh, 95
Meherrin, 3
Mims, 158, 167, 168, 183
Minton, 127, 128
Morrison, 7, 10, 11, 117, 118, 160, 166, 196, 197, 199
Moultrie, 101, 122
Mullins, 29
Mursh, 16, 83, 147

N

New River, 7, 97, 196, 198
Nickels, 29, 33
Nickens, 13

O

Office of Indian Affairs, 10, 66, 98, 188, 190
Otter, 7, 196
Oxendine, 126, 129, 130

P

Pamunkey, 16, 19, 83, 147
Parker, 65, 91, 93, 95, 181
Patterson, x, 23, 84, 87, 101, 119, 120, 122, 198, 200

Patterson, James, 119, 120
Payne, 62, 143, 145
Pee Dee, 3, 4, 8, 115, 182
Peigler, 38
Perkins, 29
Porcher, 37

Q

Quash, 7, 196, 197, 201

R

Red Head, 121
Redbones, 60
Redhead, 7, 101, 121, 122, 197
Redhead, Billey, 7
Roanoke, 3
Robbins, 13, 14, 123, 124
Robbins, Frank, 123
Roberts, 38, 39

S

Saints, 125, 177, 178
Saponi, 1, 2, 3, 6, 8
Scott, ix, 3, 7, 8, 23, 25, 41, 42, 43, 45, 83, 91, 97, 98, 101, 117, 125, 126, 127, 128, 129, 130, 131, 132, 137, 138, 147, 157, 158, 159, 160, 162, 163, 166, 168, 177, 182, 192, 197, 198, 200
Scott, Jacob, 137
Scott, John, 125, 137, 177
Seabrook, 10, 199
Shoecraft, 13

Sizemore, 29, 81, 133, 134, 135, 136
Starkey, 78, 79, 80
Stephens, 11, 21, 39, 137, 138, 199
Sumter, 1, 2, 3, 5, 7, 8, 57, 59, 60, 61, 116, 126, 129, 130, 182
Sumter County, South Carolina, 1

T

Taylor, x, 118, 139, 140, 141, 142, 143, 144, 145, 146
Tims, x, 147, 148, 149, 150
Toole, 97, 101
Tucker, 59, 61
Tutelo, 77
Tyler, x, 151, 152
Tyler, Bartlett, 151
Tyler, Betty, 151
Tyler, Nan, 151
Tyler, Priss, 151

W

Waccamaw, 8
Washington, 5, 45, 66, 79, 87, 98, 154, 163, 170, 190
Watts, x, 83, 126, 147, 153, 154, 155
Waxhaw, 3
White, 7, 23, 85, 119, 120, 126, 187, 190, 196, 197, 198
Whitesides, 23
Williamson, 186, 188, 189, 191, 192, 193, 194, 195
Williamson, George E, 193

www.ingramcontent.com/pod-product-compliance
Lightning Source LLC
Chambersburg PA
CBHW050148170426
43197CB00011B/2008